Žižek in the Clinic

A Revolutionary Proposal for a New
Endgame in Psychotherapy

Žižek in the Clinic

A Revolutionary Proposal for a New Endgame in Psychotherapy

Eliot Rosenstock

Winchester, UK
Washington, USA

JOHN HUNT PUBLISHING

First published by Zero Books, 2019
Zero Books is an imprint of John Hunt Publishing Ltd., No. 3 East St., Alresford,
Hampshire SO24 9EE, UK
office@jhpbooks.com
www.johnhuntpublishing.com
www.zero-books.net

For distributor details and how to order please visit the 'Ordering' section on our website.

Text copyright: Eliot Rosenstock 2018
Eliot Rosenstock is a Registered Associate Marriage and Family Therapist IMF95864

ISBN: 978 1 78535 925 5
978 1 78535 926 2 (ebook)
Library of Congress Control Number: 2017963699

A CIP catalogue record for this book is available from the British Library.

Design: Stuart Davies

UK: Printed and bound by CPI Group (UK) Ltd, Croydon, CR0 4YY
US: Printed and bound by Thomson-Shore, 7300 West Joy Road, Dexter, MI 48130

We operate a distinctive and ethical publishing philosophy in
all areas of our business, from our global network of authors to
production and worldwide distribution.

Contents

Special Thanks:

Dion Smotherman
Amy Ezell
Everyone in the Freud Group
Cristina

Introduction

A Žižekian Vanishing Point

Psychotherapy needs an end goal or else it is just two people in the room talking. Immediately we are faced with the problem of "why" when talking about psychotherapy. The purpose of this book is to propose a new vanishing point. In other words, what is the point on the canvas toward which the painter organizes the angle of the landscape? *The new vanishing point is this: a psychoeducated person with high insight into their own functioning with an algorithmic response process with which to respond to events on an individual microcosmic as well as a systemic level.* The goal is to help move human beings toward a position to withstand the emotional turmoil of the contemporary global capitalist value exchange market's tug on the psyche along with providing tools for every other facet of contemporary existence. The sublated individual is one who knows how external power and general systemic social structures are internalized and how the individual psyche interacts with them. In other words, if you want to surf, you must know how a wave pushes and pulls you, how desire is manufactured, where pain comes from, what is truly meaningful, what the nature of that meaning is and how that meaning should be approached.

As Jacques Lacan articulates on this phenomenon of modern manipulation of the psyche by contemporary capitalism, "We are becoming increasingly familiar with the functions of an agent (of castration). We live at a time at which we know what this conveys—fake stuff, advertising stuff, things that are there to be sold. But we also know it works this way..."[1]

New information we are exposed to is processed and made sense of by sensory inputs that are part of our own body, which we cannot fully control due to the nature of simultaneous

1

processing by our conscious and unconscious minds. Whether we are the rulers of our house[2, 3] with regards to how new information is perceived, to what degree our conscious egos have control is up for debate. It is safe to say, at the very least, there is in fact a house, a self that includes an unconscious. Early in his career, Lacan worked in a psychiatric inpatient institution. During that time, he intuited that his patients lacked the proper insight into their own psychic condition. Lacan packed patients into a church and began to lecture to them.[4] This intuition to lecture patients with psychosis is often glanced over, but it is the intuition which carries with it the potential for a contemporary Lacanian psychotherapy, which Lacan utilized for his entire career while only cursorily acknowledging it.

Lacan knew that for the psychotic he needed to provide symbolic order. It was not enough for Lacan to have a psychotic on a couch, looking up and speaking into the void, calling out to the Big Other. Lacan instinctively understood that they needed knowledge; that he would have to put himself in the University Discourse; that he would have to act as someone who held some information about what exactly truth was.

Carl Jung once stated, "Thank God I am Jung and not a Jungian." Lacan echoed a similar sentiment, "You can be Lacanian if you'd like, I myself am Freudian."[5] Despite Lacan's brilliant theoretical insights, he was at heart a Freudian analyst. Client lying back on the couch, Lacan interposing when necessary to provide an insight into a double meaning, trying to stay in the analytic discourse, the discourse Lacan insists is best for the analyst to speak to the patient in because, unlike the Master or University Discourse, the Analyst's Discourse cannot lack because the Analyst's Discourse never assumes to know.

But why does Lacan then, during his entire career, deliver lectures on the nature of the unconscious and the psyche? What then, is the purpose of this investigation if it is assumed that all new knowledge itself is some form of truth? This exchange between a colleague and a client was recently shared with me:

Therapist: "Why do you cry?"
Child: "Because I don't understand."

This is a child with behavior problems who, in addition to crying in therapy, cries throughout the day with minor provocation. What is the role that psychoeducation could play in this scenario, and specifically, Slavoj Žižek's style of Lacanian investigation into love, life and commodity fetishism? The Other for a child is at odds with the ideal Other; it is the Other with rough edges, the flat, warm Coca-Cola, versus the advertisement that shows us how to "Enjoy Coke!" Who is more under the tyranny of the superego injunction to enjoy than the child grasping for attachment to compensate for a broken home, the disembodied organ without a body, as Žižek describes the death drive? What is authority without a function inside of the family for a child?

A classic Lacanian analyst doesn't provide answers, championing small gains the client builds through speaking to Big Other as they throw out master signifiers. "Unless we define happiness in a rather sad way, namely that it is to be like everyone else, which is what the autonomous ego could be resolved into—nobody, it must be said, knows what it is."[6] But let us think back to Lacan's intuition at the institution. He gave credit to the institutionalized to be able to cognitively understand his teachings, and that his teachings would somehow better them. What is it that draws people to Lacan in the modern era? It is the idea that psychoeducation can provide depth and meaning, not unlike the function of psychotherapy for a depressed child. We can psychoeducate a child on why their friends aren't perfect (aren't object ideals); we can revisit with them how they repeat these ideals and it causes them pain. In the institutionalized psychotic, the repeating scenarios matched up against the ideal self and values of the client can be rationalized.

Dialectics can be formed with any client: The internal values of the client, with event. Where these come together and where they do not, parallaxes can be mapped. A Hegelian-Lacanian topology is cognitively mapped. The client will often seem as if they suddenly "click into place," like they suddenly have a pathway forward. This is not done with psychoanalysis, but with the psychoeducational narratives in the way Lacanian discourse was originally intuited to work by Lacan in the institution, and by Žižek in front of the audience.

So, what is this book and what is it not? This book **is** a description of the toolbox I've crafted as a psychotherapist which contains a variety of ways in which the Žižekian mode of investigation into psychic phenomena can be utilized in the clinical setting. This book **is not** a book advocating a specific modality of therapy, nor is it a book suggesting the superiority of psychotherapy over psychoanalysis. This book **is** an inside look into the therapeutic profession meant for lay-fans of philosophy and psychotherapists of every model, and a description of the intrinsic closing of lack or distance between the subject's split sense of identity, and how it is different to intrinsic analytic models. This book **is not** a book by an expert in Lacanian psychoanalysis, but rather a practicing psychodynamic psychotherapist working with, but not an expert in, the Lacanian model. By psychotherapy, I mean two people, the therapist and the client, in two chairs facing each other, as opposed to the speaking-to-the-wall, hyper-free-associative nature of psychoanalysis. By expert, I mean someone who has worked extensively under Lacanians and has been practicing for many years within this type of supervision and framework. While my supervisors allow me to work from a Lacanian perspective, this does not make me an expert in "Lacanian psychotherapy," which is a protected term. This book **is,** in its limited capacity, a practical guide to how I have managed to integrate ideas of Slavoj Žižek's psychoanalytic philosophy from the lecture hall and public forum into the "two people talking to each other" clinical setting, producing an outcome which we can term positive.

Chapter 1

A New Dialectic

Nothing created appears without urgency; nothing in urgency fails to surpass itself in speech.
Jacques Lacan, Ecrits[7]

What is psychotherapy, and more importantly, why does psychotherapy exist? "The what" cannot be answered without "the why;" and thus, "the why" is the primordial form of "the what." All models of psychotherapy are variations of two people sitting in a room, in various positions, talking to each other in an attempt to produce a unique effect that causes one of the two people to negate their current psychic condition in some manner. Lacan pulls up his chair and calls out to us, the audience he would never know, and states, "You're ready to hear this, which moreover is a truth that's always been well known, but which has never been given its rightful place – inasmuch as desire enters the fray of love and is one of its major stakes, desire doesn't pertain to the loved object."[8] The dialectic between the therapist and the client is the core of the discussion of modality, and what constitutes modality, and what exactly the ideology of the modality should be. It is seemingly self-evident that there should be a subject-supposed-to-know to some degree in the therapist or analyst, because to enter a contract with a client/patient with no direction is unethical. But how much is the therapist supposed to know?

This is where behavioral psychology has closed "the lack" of ambiguity in the client and argues that "the solution to this dilemma may be found in an obvious, yet substantially neglected area: the rich data available in the person's conscious ideas and in his common-sense ways of defining and coping with his psychological problems."[9] To Aaron Beck's argument that conscious thought is the disregarded content of psychotherapy, there is a parallel to be drawn with the objectivist (Ayn Rand) philosophy of the business man as the oppressed minority. The business man's motivations may not be as fully examined as the motivations of those experiencing extreme poverty, but to ignore the needs of those in extreme poverty as a reaction to a presumed lack of knowledge of the bureaucratic mechanisms of industry is a ridiculous solution.

In the same way, Aaron Beck's suggestion that the conscious mind is oppressed by a Freudian obsession with the unconscious is unhelpful, in that the word a client uses in the room is conscious content, which can be a gateway to the unconscious. As explained in Lacan's lecture "From Anal to Ideal" in the Anxiety Seminar Collection, "In dealing with the anal, people think they're getting closer to the matter, quite literally, to the concrete underpinnings. They think they are demonstrating that we know how to account even for life's more disagreeable aspects."[10] We are overloaded by our conscious thoughts, and our unconscious content influences our conscious thoughts. To deny the necessity of examining what could be present in the unconscious is to eliminate a key part of the dialectic process of psychotherapy, the dynamic relationship between the conscious and the unconscious.

The current behavioral models of psychotherapy are reactionary negations of the abstractions and esoteric properties of psychoanalysis and depth psychology. While the modern behavioral approaches embrace much of the liberating spirit that makes the therapeutic process revolutionary the various behavioral models, such as Rational Emotive Behavior Therapy (REBT), Cognitive Behavior Therapy (CBT), and Dialectical Behavior Therapy (DBT) are a necessary part of the historical march to a more effective, liberating model of psychotherapy. By "liberating," I mean a true sense of personal empowerment and accomplishment, rather than an empty lack of symbolic boundaries in a single instance of ecstatic knowing; in essence I am suggesting there is an approach to phenomenon that psychotherapy can create, an algorithm of approach that is "better" than the unexamined mind.

As opposed to earlier Hegelians, Žižek's spirit-inducing savoir, which integrates Hegel, has the benefit of being influenced by decades of psychoanalytic theory. As Žižek writes in *Event*, "Spirit is itself the wound it tries to heal, that is, the wound is self-inflicted. What is 'Spirit' at its most elementary? The 'wound' of nature: the spirit of human subjectivity is the power of differentiating, of 'abstracting,' of tearing apart and treating as free-standing what in reality is part of an organic unity."[11] Both Žižek and early Hegelians hint at some sort of state that is both beyond and within reality, both an escape and a hyper-examination that allows for some sort of becoming that does not escape ideology, but at least to some degree has a self that knows the game which the mind is playing and is not fooling itself.

If the unconscious existed fully outside the self and was available as a living human, I cannot imagine how in any society the unconscious would be tolerated without being thrown into prison or publicly executed. It is no wonder that the behaviorists have found that destroying the unconscious within a theoretical framework has very positive benefits, for the unconscious is closer to a war criminal than a saint. For many people suffering from psychosis, whose unconscious is not processed against a society that is beneficial to some degree, it is violent in its untamed wilderness of the unknown, and as soon as the unconscious is known, it is no longer the unconscious but information held in the conscious mind. The logical question that follows is: what exactly is in the unconscious that should be negated as unconscious and should be brought into the conscious frame? All psychotherapy is a negation of something as unconscious material, and bringing it into the clinic room in one form or another, always incomplete, always lacking, but always negating the aspect's unconscious nature.

This process brings us to the question, what is it that Žižek teaches us that Lacan doesn't? The especially Hegelian view of Lacan, one that believes the approach to new stimuli will be a dialectic, one that utilizes the conscious mind. Technocapital is flowing at hyperspeed and is primed to grab onto our drives and pull us toward capitalistic integration into the will of the Other; therefore, now more than ever, we as a species need a conscious psychoeducation.

What is the difference between psychology and the Freudian tradition, between psychology and Hegelian philosophy? What is the philosophical angle to analysis and why is it necessary? Philosophy can exist in a disembodied state which floats freely on any sort of subject. One can hypothesize about the nature of phenomenology and object without it relating back to a subject's felt state. A Hegelian deconstruction of the various forms of negation and description of an object in space-time doesn't quite rely on any one individual or their motivations in the same way psychoanalysis does and, in fact, derides recognizing the symbolic order as empty as "accordingly evil" and "subjective emptiness."[12] Psychotherapy relies on hypotheses of feeling, of a person, of an existing state.

To dialectically analyze the individual with the systems which they inhabit without providing a moral absolute such as Hegel does is what is necessary, because psychotherapy is ultimately for the benefit of the mental health of the individual; thus, any therapeutic dialectic that is crafted that accounts for the purpose of psychotherapy, which is for the mental health of the individual therapeutic subject. This is not enough however; specificity of what this dialectic should consist of must be outlined and should be foundationally laid out in the material reality of the psyche. This material reality is outlined first by Freud, with additions and negations to this very day. Every addition is also a negation, and thus some additions have negated the material reality of the psyche. The fact that philosophy can be somewhat split into analytic philosophy and continental philosophy illustrates that there are multiple forms of analysis of reality. One school more narrative, one school more structural, but analytics and continentals are both structural in the sense that they attempt to access some primordial essence of being. If this is so, the unconscious content is always there within any of these investigations. Analytic philosophy has subtext and cannot escape the nature of the unconscious and underlying meaning. Wittgenstein writes, "…when I uttered the double negation, what constituted my meaning it as a strengthened negative and not as an affirmative? There is no answer running: 'It consisted in the fact that….' In certain circumstances, instead of saying, 'This duplication is meant as a strengthening,' I can *pronounce* it as a strengthening."[13] Is this not the attempt to bring the unconscious into conscious reality? Why is there the attempt to bring this unconscious into consciousness? Why was Wittgenstein carried away with writing his investigations into the meaning of the framework of language? As posited at the beginning of this chapter, we cannot know "the what" if we don't know "the why." "the why" is the primordial "the what", and when we don't know why, we don't know what. Human beings venture into the unknown to discover new ground, but new ground for what? If they are venturing into the unknown, it goes without saying there is something besides the unknown, and that is the place from which humans embark. Why do they go into the unknown, but to bridge the gap between the known and the unknown? The process of interacting with this gap can be referred to as the dialectic which psychotherapy and philosophy work with.

What should constitute a new dialectic then? On what ground should we embark into the unknown? What is the relationship to the unknown that a human being should have? What is the process of interacting with the known and the unknown? A new

Žižekian influenced psychotherapeutic dialectic should exist from an accurate framework involving a metaphysical frame of what knowledge can and cannot do; but most importantly, how knowledge relates to the psyche and the human experience of love, suffering and everything that is more or less. To say "everything else in between," rather than "more or less" would fundamentally miss the point by substituting colloquial phrasing for truth. Precision is important because this is a philosophical/ psychological search for a framework that works most positively in that agreed upon setting, and for meaning that differentiates individual psychology from philosophy in the first place: two people, in a room, sitting or lying or more rarely standing in various positions. One takes the role of therapist, and focuses on somehow improving the existence in some way of the person taking on the role of "client."

This ideal goal, being so full of subjectivity in the realm of what constitutes improvement of the life of the client, is why it is important that the theoretical groundwork be consciously mapped by **both the therapist and the client.** The client, with the dialectic process in mind, can build an idea of "the why" and get a grip on "the what." The child in the introduction, who cries and states out loud it is "because I don't understand," is capable of an accurate analysis of her[his] own misery, one that would be difficult, if not impossible, for an older client to formulate into such a precise encapsulation. The older client knows, or perhaps thinks that he knows too much. But knows too much about what? And when one says "what," one must once again, realize "the why."

Understanding always lacks, but what does it lack? In essence, the child is crying, because they do not understand. This does not mean to grasp for the impossible totality of the master, but to have a signifier from which to make a foundation to build a psyche inside oneself that one would rather live with than one's previous state of existence.

Chapter 2

The Psychodynamic Implications of Žižek's Parallax View

...if, for Lacan, there is no sexual relationship, then, for Marxism proper, there is no relationship between economy and politics, no "meta-language" enabling us to grasp the two levels from the same neutral standpoint—or, rather, because —these two levels are inextricably intertwined [. . .] It is no wonder the structure of this impossible relationship is that of the Moebius Strip: first, we have to progress from the political spectacle to its economic infrastructure; then, in the second step, we have to confront the irreducible dimension of the political struggle at the very heart of the economy.

Slavoj Žižek[14]

What is at stake when one goes into the room of a therapist's office? Happiness may be a tempting answer, but it is an extremely incomplete answer. The client in the room with a psychotherapist may not be there because they want to be happier. In fact, some clients who seek therapy may describe themselves as happy people for the most part, only wishing to negate negative aspects of themselves, such as addictive behaviors affecting themselves and people around them, or a wish to get rid of anxiety, or perhaps flashbacks from trauma. Even with these few examples, it is easy to see that happiness is an incomplete answer.

Is there a complete answer then? No, but there is a universally true answer: the movement of the psyche from where it is to somewhere else. This involves the necessity of understanding the libidinal economy of the conscious/unconscious dialectic. But how can we understand this economy? Žižek writes on the impossibility of singularizing the traditional economic economy:

> Today, we experience cyberspace as a new transparent artificial life-world whose icons simulate our everyday reality—and this new environment is by definition uncontrollable, it displays an opacity of its own, we never master it, we perceive it as a fragment of a larger universe; our proper attitude toward it is therefore not a programmatic mastery but a bricolage, improvising, finding our way through its impenetrable density."[15]

The concept of the parallax attempts to describe the impossibility of an enlightenment model of a total picture. The impulse of the psychotherapist to totalize into a singular framework is a tempting one. Freud does it with libido; modern behaviorists do it with simple models to explain behavior that does not account for the unconscious; other therapists give up on the whole endeavor of understanding the psyche and instead give their clients tools based on need. Use "tool a" to reduce anxiety. Use "tool b" when you feel like life isn't worth living. Use "tool c" if you want to dump ravioli on your father's head at dinner time. A disclaimer should be added to this criticism, in that these psychic tools are not entirely ineffective. Building a tool box for reducing pathological symptomology is an effective way to circumvent the cause and "the why" of a client's symptom, which for many reasons psychology clinics often times find preferable. Neo-brief-therapy arrives from the future as insurance companies manage to reterritorialize the human psyche into something singular yet unrecognizable as having any meaning, while the unconscious content struggles to get a grip. [16] Capitalism, with the help of technology expanding flows of information to the point of symbolic order disintegration, erodes the foundational reference points of psychotherapy. Capital recapturing the system of the psychotherapy industry ensures that the main goal of client improvement for client improvement sake is replaced by goals that are more marketable, such as fewer bad feelings or a better-behaved child for your parental dollar investment. Progress that isn't immediately understood by a lay person may be tossed aside as unimportant, but these complex concepts simply are not unimportant. This is a negation that must be negated, and the lack of foundational knowledge regarding the nature of one's own psyche is why the psychoeducational style of Žižek's Hegelian Lacan is a necessary foundational tool for the continued progress of psychotherapy.

It is necessary to embrace a form of dialectic rather than pursue "detachment from material reality,"[17] which is especially dangerous in its appeal to the lay person. The archetype of the Buddhist master is pervasive in the therapy profession, as various gurus with MAs and PhDs advertise themselves as harbingers of this general idea of wellness. Certain aspects of clinics are made to suggest calmness and tranquility. Tranquility is seen as an ideal endpoint, and those who cannot achieve this Western Buddhist model of tranquility may be labeled as malcontents of some degree or another. Bringing real-world situations and dialectics into the room with a client is antithetical to the client facing down his or her feelings with a calming shaman in the therapy room, causing the client to be overcome with validation. There is always the danger de-escalation will replace active engagement with reality in a similar manner to the marijuana and video games model of self-care. What then, is the nature of the tools that are based on a rational foundational therapeutic algorithm that can be given to the client, and what do they consist of? Lacan writes of the idea of finding meaningful sites in the topological map:

> It is surprising that an underground cavern was chosen. Such a site only creates obstacles to the viewing that one assumes is presupposed by the creation and observation of the striking

images which decorate the walls. The production of images and their viewing could not have been easy given the forms of lighting available to primitive men. Yet in the beginning those paintings that we take to be the earliest productions of primitive art were thrown up on the walls of a cavern. One could call them tests in both senses of the word, subjective and objective. Tests no doubt for the artist, for, as you know, these images are often painted over each other; it's as if in a consecrated spot it represented, for each subject capable of undertaking such an exercise, the opportunity to draw or project afresh what he needed to bear witness to, and to do so moreover over what had already been done before.[18]

Once again to find "the what," we should return to "the why." Current therapy modalities do not consider this deep time, this re-painting of the cave. Buddhism, existentialism and capitalism all meld together in a traffic jam which further makes opaque the essential quality of the dialectic between the conscious and unconscious mind, which ultimately results in a general goal of de-escalating the symptom as having an adverse effect. If master signifiers are unable to be identified because there is a fear of approaching the places where the sinthome is tied into place, if we are afraid of asking about repeated motifs and instead focus on avoiding repetition, a large chunk of the psychotherapeutic process is negated and replaced with something that can only be called an empty shell version of the foundational psychoanalytic experience.

Sartre summates this modern ideology which entangles itself with the ideology of colonial capitalism and surplus enjoyment in the name of product placement extremely well with his Coca-Cola-esque statement that has mass appeal for the demographic of this ideology:

We want freedom for freedom's sake and in every particular

circumstance. And in wanting freedom we discover that it depends entirely on the freedom of others, and that the freedom of others depends on ours [...] Therefore, in the name of this will of freedom, which freedom itself implies, I may pass judgment on those who seek to hide [from] themselves the complete arbitrariness and complete freedom of their existence.[19]

Without rehashing Žižek's well-known critique of freedom as a concept, one can build on it to demonstrate how this concept of freedom that Žižek critiques has insidiously weaved its way into the folds of psychotherapy in the form of a parallax mapping. Freedom reaches its limit when meaning is unable to be produced due to a misconception of the nature of being. The agoraphobic may feel free in their choice to stay inside against the wishes of the Other. Meaning is unable to be produced when legality and empty symbolic order are seen as utterly useless symbolic order. This is the unconscious nihilism, the void of the existentialist, that cognitive modeling runs away from and into the meaning that is capable of being produced by a person's conscious thoughts. However, if the dialectic is not formed between a human being and their unconscious, leading to an understanding of their unconscious, the conscious thoughts of humans, are simply inaccurate.

A general theme of transcendence in the form of escape twists its way in through the seemingly innocuous positivity and truisms of humanist psychotherapy. The overall message of the toolkit model of psychotherapy is that the problem is the anxiety, depression or other negative emotion, and this feeling can be transcended through a more positive, or at the very least, a more realistic outlook. With this second idea, I completely agree, a more realistic outlook is needed. But the idea of "a realistic outlook" in and of itself tells us nothing about what that outlook should be. In object relations, a realistic outlook is recognizing the good and the bad in things and seeing things not as all good and all bad. In Dialectical Behavioral Therapy, the realistic outlook is something that involves both emotion and intellect, not letting one rule over the other. These are both answers, and what we need is not an answer, but rather a better way to question. The way this is done is by building with the client an understanding of the parallax view, and an examination of the primordial wall in which different paintings keep being painted on. It is easy to get caught up on the paintings of this Lacanian primordial caveman wall, as the paintings are the conscious end goal of painting. But then why the specific wall, what is the story behind the set of all the paintings on that specific wall?

Chapter 3

Living in Uncertainty

The Difficulty of Contradicting Oneself

[. . .] No one who is in pain conceives it as a privilege, but the privilege of pain, according to Hegel, stems from its contradictory status. To be in pain is to find oneself immersed in contradiction [. . .] Why is pain the "concrete existence" of contradiction? Most of us, when we experience pain, do not think of it as a contradictory experience. But Hegel conceives pain here as the negation of living entity: it is a response to stimulations that damage and even threaten to destroy the entity.

Todd McGowan[20]

To bring the idea of uncertainty and conflict into the modern era, we can regard the idea of crafting an algorithm for new information as shorthand for what the endpoint of psychotherapy can achieve. Lacan writes, "In a certain fashion, one could say that the Hegelian dialectic of the conflict of consciousness is after all nothing other than this attempt at elaborating the whole world of human knowledge starting from a pure conflict which is radically imaginary and radically destructive in its origin." [21] What is a non-destructive conflict origin? Is there such a thing in a Hegelian world of negated negations which are once more negated? A psychotherapeutic model that gives the patient an algorithm to approach new events and stimuli that aren't designed solely as a method to lower the anxiety, depression mania, paranoid thinking or other form of adverse reaction an event creates certainly would be destructive to the order of tool-based psychotherapy. Psychoanalysis negates reactionary value systems being seen as the end-all psychological good; cognitive approaches negate psychotherapy and the disavowal of the objective conscious thought; the return to Lacan and the proposal of a Hegelian-Lacanian system is where we must once more negate the negated negation.

Existence doesn't happen in a vacuum, nor is it a straight line, but an intertwined tangle of internal and external factors. Freud writes the following on this phenomenon regarding dreams: "The second half of the dream therefore represented thoughts [...] that belonged to the first half of the underlying latent content; the first half of the dream corresponded with the second half of the latent content [...]Besides this inversion in order, further inversions took place in each half of the dream."[22] New information gathered is only relevant when measured against a why, and these whys are not always conscious. But, through conscious effort toward understanding the nature of these conflicts, one can have a wider understanding of the nature of oneself, and of one's own pain. Referring to the child who is in pain because they do not understand, one has to ask, "what is understanding?"

Because understanding always lacks the flows, images, sounds and other sensory stimuli exposed to the client in their day-to-day life in the form of recognized language, it is an impossible task to set forth for a client to understand consciously all new information and its effect on them. However, one can develop in the client an understanding of understanding itself.

Reality stabilizes itself when some fantasy-frame of a 'symbolic bliss' forecloses the view into the abyss of the Real. Far from being a kind of figment of our dreams that prevents us from 'seeing reality as it effectively is,' fantasy is constitutive of what we call reality [...] In other words, the price we pay for our access to 'reality' is that something – the reality of the trauma – must be 'repressed.'[23]

If one is to examine the material quality and implications of this idea, **the therapist has the capacity to choose what becomes repressed when beginning to examine the psychic content of a client and then chooses how to approach it.** For example, when a therapist asks a client to go over their dream a second time and asks them to expound on a specific forgotten variable, the other variables and contents may in fact be forced under into the unconscious.

If one were to perform a cultural meta-analysis on Žižek as event himself, one could demonstrate what an understanding of understanding entails. Marxism changes with each separate cultural and sociopolitical climate, in order to react to the material conditions a particular people are facing. In the same way, Žižek makes use of Lacan in an era which Lacan has missed, the hyper-information age of the internet. The nature of the virtual has taken on another meaning besides symbol; the virtual now has its own plane of existence that is publicly recognized as virtual reality. If this new material condition is ignored, new developments in Lacanian theory will be missed. If Žižek is ignored, then the material condition of Žižek himself will be sublated into those who study Lacan. If Žižek's work is valuable and is only being suppressed because of Žižek's status as a philosopher who is popular, then this is no reason at all to ignore Žižek's contributions. The point of this dialectic is to raise the question, "to what degree, is Žižek himself, or Hegel or Lacan, in our mindset?" How does our reaction to Žižek reflect on how we see new bearers of older information? Or, by negating the importance of Žižek, do we once again paint over the cave painting as did the ancient cave dwellers described by Lacan? The dialectic of the event of Žižek is itself a flux between being-non-entity and Roark-esque fountainhead. Without this process of dialectic exchange between a Lacanian analyst and their Other while out in public, to what extent does a Lacanian analyst understand his reactions to the stimuli, "Slavoj Žižek". It has an undercurrent of nihilistic meaninglessness behind it, a supposition that all dialectic processes are meaningless and that the true essence is how a reaction affects a client's feelings and surroundings.

This lack in the process of the dialectic exchange required for a thorough investigation into the psyche has been taken advantage of by various cognitivists in proposing psychological systems which state explicitly that the unconscious is something which does not exist. Whether or not the active deniers of unconscious content truly believe unconscious content is non-existent is uncertain, but for all intents-and-purposes this does not matter. In the therapy room, should not a client be allowed to decide whether or not their anger at a situation is healthy through a rational process? If there is no algorithm but the presupposed algorithm of "contain the negative," this fails because the negative is a false category insofar as it is not a totalizing one. The system which I propose in the final chapter of this text is not a totalizing proposal of a rationale that a client will generate, but it creates a new endpoint for the client in that it gives one the ability to discern for oneself how to interact with new stimuli by giving them the eyes to approach in a Žižekian manner the nature of the event.

Event as a Žižekian concept is something that relates to a thrusting of the status quo into the unknown. At times event is an Armageddon-like fall or destruction. In the psyche, this catastrophizing of event can be interpreted as anxiety. Lacan writes: "Anxiety, Freud taught us, plays the role of a signal function in relation to something. I say that it's a signal in relation to what occurs in connection with the subject's relation to the object in all its generality. The subject is only ever able to enter this relation within the vacillation of a certain fading, the same that the notation barred S designates. Anxiety is the signal of certain movements of this relation."[24]

An event can be seen as a raising of a signifier to a master signifier, or something that was once known, now contains great meaning. The addition of meaning in a strictly Hegelian sense, is also destructive of what the signifier was previously. A new theorist in a university negates the standing of the old theorists. A son negates the father with his birth, and aggression travels both ways, forming the Oedipal submission-to or destruction-of the father in the intrapsychic space.

Oedipus rears his head again to be painted over by the cavemen. Our current incarnation of humanity has the benefit of knowledge accumulation and of information flow, which is also humanity's contemporary mortal challenge. Exposed to a tidal wave of desire manufactured by the internet, only proper psychoeducation regarding this overflow of manufactured drive can create a savoir for those who are made anxious by the new outpouring of capital-tainted information in our contemporary techno sphere.

Chapter 4

The Master is the Provider of Convenience

There is no other meaning to the conservation of energy than this mark of an instrumentation that signifies the power of the master.
Jacques Lacan[25], Seminar 17

Convenience rules the consumer with a much stronger grip than it rules industry. Industry will have pushback against over-automation of industries. Workers protest; politicians protect inefficient methods that safeguard the interests of their backers or populace. This means that there is a decent amount of monetary incentive for the ruling class to provide resistance to assimilation into the most efficient means available. The individual consumer does not have anything near to a similar system protection against automation. The unconscious master signifier of the technology industry is that the easier things are for us, the better it is. There is an imposition of truth which suggests that the consumer is obligated: "For truth, as it happens, makes this signifier 'death' appear[...]Truth has more than one face[...] truth is experienced, this does not at all mean that it thereby knows [connait] any more about the real..."[26] What is the death drive that is imposed on the individual subject? That they must desire something. What must they desire? In essence, the subject must desire more. **What must they desire more of** is the question, and it's a question that needs to be addressed, yet is simply glanced over by modern behavioral methodologies.

DBT came into being as somewhat of a miracle cure because suddenly, untreatable patients began to become treatable. The person with Borderline Personality Disorder in the Diagnostic and Statistical Manual (DSM) IV was labeled an "Axis II" diagnosis because it was originally thought that there was nothing that could be done against the immovable personality. DBT is a newer phenomenon than CBT and REBT, the latter two having ushered the therapy profession into a new era of ego psychology and non-recognition of the unconscious.

The glory and the danger of the DBT model is that it is truly successful at treating the symptoms of Borderline Personality Disorder. Suddenly people afflicted with Borderline Personality Disorder, whose moods were leading them to self-harm and even suicide, could adjust their relationship to their initial impulses of anxiety, rage and overwhelming sadness. Suddenly the disorder termed Borderline Personality Disorder seemed curable.

The question we should ask is, "is this all that matters?" In Marsha Linehan's latest update to her theory workbook, there is a wonderful and amusingly forceful tool to direct the intensity of the DBT client's will into pure egoistic capital. In one of her various "Interpersonal Effectiveness" worksheets and handouts, Linehan begins a remarkably Lacanian styled *Che Vuoi*,[27] suggesting to the therapized subject the following assessment methods: "**1. CAPABILITY**: Is this person able to give you what you want? If YES, raise the intensity of ASKING. Do you have what the person wants? If NO, raise the intensity of NO." In addition, "**8. GIVE AND TAKE**: What have you done for the person? Are you giving at least as much as you ask for...Do you owe this person a favor? Does he or she do a lot for you? If NO raise the intensity of NO."[28] One could simply make a leftist critique of reducing the value of the Other into a purely material assessment of their worth to you, and then what is the best way to become the master in relation to the Other? However, there is one flaw that is not moralistic. The flaw in this outlook in relation to the Other is what is missing before step one is not an answer, but a question. How do you know what you want, why do you want it, are there some variations of this question that are overlooked?

DBT is like other behavior therapies in that it attempts to

circumvent the unconscious by using various tools that can be employed without getting into any complex explanations of the way the psyche works. This would be useful, except it still leaves the therapized subject adrift, with the illusion of control by putting the therapized subject into the master's discourse. "What is there to conceal? That, as soon as the father enters the field of the master's discourse where we are in the process of orientating ourselves, he is, from the origins, castrated."[29] The subject that does not know its own limit is more vulnerable than the subject that knows what it can and cannot do.

The dialectic that DBT proposes is one between intellect and emotion. This is an incomplete analysis of the psyche, but it is designed to be incomplete. When one does not try to parse out the contents of the unconscious, one has no room for error. When one does not try to figure out the nature of drives, one is limited to only playing games with the secondary aspects of the end results of "The Lacanian field," as Lacan names the integrated nature of destruction and sexual drives in seminar 17. "I have already said enough to you for you to know that jouissance is the jar of Danaides,[30] and that once you have started, you never know where it will end. It begins with a tickle and ends in a blaze of petrol. That's always what jouissance is."[31]

DBT can be summed up in Lacanian terms as the art of making sure the tickle does not turn into a blaze of petrol. This is an extremely useful tool that Marsha Linehan has created, and she deserves to be praised for the way in which the application of this petrol blaze reduction modality has helped people live healthier day-to-day lives. Yet one has to ask, what is causing the tickle in the first place? Why is this question going completely unexamined? There is a fear of examining the root causes of pain. Avoidance behavior surrounding these root causes might have functional properties for a patient in urgent need of coping tools, but what does it mean for the rest of the populace who are not in extremis? Utilizing tools that only reduce symptoms after the initial reaction means that the therapized subject is constantly playing catch-up to what is alien to themselves in the Other. In other words, symptomatic approaches to psychotherapy give the illusion of actualizing the patient while falling short of truly providing the therapized subject with the answer to his anger. The answer becomes an explanation of secondary rather than primary phenomena. The subject in this state is ripe for exploitation by forces that regulate emotion.

In the famous pop psychology book *How to Win Friends and Influence People*, Dale Carnegie writes:

In a Nutshell

Six ways to make people like you:

PRINCIPLE 1: Become genuinely interested in other people.

PRINCIPLE 2: Smile.

PRINCIPLE 3: Remember that a person's name is to that person the sweetest and most important sound in any language.

PRINCIPLE 4: Be a good listener. Encourage others to talk about themselves.

PRINCIPLE 5: Talk in terms of the other person's interests.

PRINCIPLE 6: Make the other person feel important – and do it sincerely.[32]

It's very important that we do not neglect to glance over the implications of these statements. There is a habit in professional circles to ignore the battery of signifiers that a title of a theory suggests in an attempt to create precise definitions.

It is not a coincidence that the book entitled *How to Win Friends and Influence People* has quite a bit of information about how to regulate the emotional temperature of other people. When an algorithm provides to the subject convenience, that algorithm has control over you as a subject. The subject is no longer paddling, but being pushed by a current. The algorithmic good of emotional regulation makes one forget what one truly values outside of emotional regulation. *The necessity of a Žižekian vanishing point is the necessity of being able to break out of trances that one is put into by forces only designed to exploit the subject, such as algorithmic advertising, news stories designed to use the illusion of ease or naturalness to influence policy, and personal use of other people's convenience provision as a way to become the Master.* Contemporary capitalism has incurred a sea change; rather than "might makes right," society becomes "ease makes right."

What is the downside to the reduction of emotional temperature becoming the de facto measuring stick of the agency of a modality? "(The master) gives a sign, the master signifier, and everybody jumps. That's where you must start, which is in effect, completely impossible...whatever the signs, whatever the master signifiers that come to be inscribed in the place of the agent, under no circumstances will production have a relationship to truth."[33] The relaxation and immovability of a subject becomes the determiner of the moral correctness of a position. A questioning of any sort of dogma becomes due to the master signifier of placid emotional response, incorrect if it bothers too many people. If truth is an agreement between large numbers of people not to bother each other too much, then what becomes of any sort of statement or proposal that might ruffle the feathers of many people? In this environment of emotional placidity as the ultimate agent of truth, those who state they are grievously unregulated by any discourse become the ultimate determiners of what it is and is not permissible to talk about. The result is that various members of society are now, more than ever, susceptible to having their mistrust of the alien "Other" exploited by politicians and corporations utilizing technocapital with total disregard for an individual subject's mental health.

Chapter 5

How-To-Hegelese for the Everyday American

The working class is thus split into three, each part with its own 'way of life' and ideology: the enlightened hedonism and liberal multiculturalism of the intellectual class, the populist fundamentalism of the working class, and in the more extreme, singular forms of the outcast fraction. [34] *In Hegelese, this triad is clearly the triad of the universal (intellectual workers), particular (manual workers), and singular (outcasts)...The proletariat is thus divided into three, each part played off against the others: intellectual labourers full of cultural prejudices against the 'redneck' workers; workers who display a populist hatred of intellectuals and outcasts; outcasts who are antagonistic to a society as such. The old call of 'Proletarians, unite!' is thus more pertinent than ever: in the new conditions of 'post-industrial' capitalism, the unity of the three fractions of the working class is already their victory.*
Slavoj Žižek, How to Begin from the Beginning[35]

The title of this chapter is not meant to exclude citizens of other countries, but to emphasize the level of workable discourse to which Hegelian concepts need to be brought to make them more accessible. It is, in fact, possible to bring the algorithmic style of Hegelian discernment from therapist to client using even my unsavory dialect, of American-English. Ignoring that it is unethical to tell a client, "read Hegel," such a telling also would be ineffective. In addition to the analysis of history, mind and law contained in Hegel's writings, there is woven through all of these an important psychological tool; Hegel's own algorithmic approach to raw material and abstract problems. For instance, "When you do something new, you take away what was there before," or, "when you stop doing something, you add an entirely new set of things that you do," as a process to describe negation. This can be applied in a variety of ways when working with a client's conscious and unconscious content because motive that seems to be split by the client in an object relations sense (all good) as only additive or vaguely positive has to be looked at as a negation. This Hegelian notion is an essential component for the client to truly understand their motives.

The events within the client's life can be looked at with a similar method of discernment: a set of abstract problems that need to be approached from a number of different angles. The dialectic between the conscious and the unconscious, that is embedded in the process of psychotherapy and psychoanalysis, allows the unfolding of the questions that the client needs to approach in her quest for a life that is, in her estimation, "better" than when she came in. This is not the same as happier, and not the same as "more meaningful," but a question posed to the therapist about providing of partially defined, "better." The therapist has a vague idea of what better can be. The idea of a simple reduction in negative emotion is a very tempting place to end in the search for this abstract notion of "better." But more than just not in pain, the client needs to be given a way to extract meaning and purpose from their environment. This requires more than just Linehan's wise-mind algorithmic determination tools, although those tools are significant in that through their use, Linehan brought the dialectic process into the mainstream, insurance-approved field of psychotherapy.

The response of the child in the introduction to the question of why she/he cries, "because I don't understand," is an important reminder of what needs to be processed by the self to create this idea of "better." It is not only self-knowledge that a client needs, but knowledge of how to process new information. Hegel states in his Phenomenology of Mind, "With self-consciousness, then, we have now passed into the native land of truth, into that kingdom where it is at home."[36] This translation of Hegel may seem to be very much like many saccharine truisms about knowing one's self that we hear today, but a closer examination illuminates proto-psychoanalytical elements to this statement. There is an acknowledgment of a hierarchy, a kingdom, that is only valid with a particular ordering. To understand what is the self, we must be able to investigate the dynamics in relation to what is alien to the self, *the Other.*

Lacan explains the concept of the self and other in *Ecrits* thusly: "It is in the specific reality of *interpersonal relations* that a psychology can define its own object and its method of investigation. The concepts implied by this object and this method are not subjective, but *relativistic.*"[37] There can be a nihilistic response to the acknowledgment of relativism, but the relativistic outlook of interpersonal signifying chains is not only materially important, but 100 percent demonstrable to any client, no matter their socio-economic status or political viewpoint.

If a client has ever been in school, they know that there is a dynamic between the student and teacher that is not one of absolute equality. Even if one has the most permissive teacher possible, the teacher can determine the coursework which outlines the overall environment of the student. In less permissive settings, it is more probable that a student would have at least one strict teacher they didn't get along with at least once in their academic career; there is an even more apparent demonstration of power relations between the client and the holder of truth. Being able to materially demonstrate the client's own topological position in their current micro-social power relations is the first step toward demonstrating their place in larger systems. There are various tools that involve a dialectic between the unconscious and conscious that one can use, classic free-association being one of the oldest, as an example. The information gathered via psychotherapy includes client history with figures in authority, and people who the client simply believes they, or materially actually do, have authority over. The process of psychotherapy consists in part of gathering information from the client, which the therapist is not necessarily doing anything with immediately.

In my clinical practice, I created a tool which was given the ethically proper supervisor blessing to parse out the client's relationship to power dynamics, in general and abstractly with various "other" power relations outside the client's ego self, with an exercise I call, "What Did the...." There are five chess pieces set up in a pentagon:

1) the pawn
2) the knight
3) the rook (explained as, "This is the castle, 'the rook.'")
4) the queen
5) the king

After the pieces and their value are explained to the client, the process goes like this: "What did the pawn say to the knight?" (client answers) "What did the knight say to the rook?" (client answers), and so on until most of the combinations of piece questions are asked. Answers that the client glances over by not giving a reasonably full answer ("Hello," for example), or if the client pauses for an extended period and seems to be at a loss for words, are focused on. For instance, if the client has trouble with the queen, a series of questions is asked involving the queen.

The pawn symbolizes a subject under the influence of an authority. The knight is both subjugated and has authority. The rook is a piece representing foundational structure. The queen is a female (possibly maternal) authority and the king is a male (possibly paternal) authority. These are not abstract, made up relationships to each other, but a small replication of power dynamics that the client observes or experiences and has a psychical relationship to. Claude Levi-Strauss writes about the subject's relationship to transference stand-ins in *Totemism:*

Before a recourse to anxiety could supply even the outlines of an explanation, we should have to know what anxiety actually is, and then what relations exist between on the one hand, a confused and disordered emotion, and on the other, acts marked by the most rigorous precision and which are divided into a number of distinct categories. By what mechanism might the former give rise to the latter? Anxiety is not a cause: it is the way in which man perceives, subjectively and obscurely, an internal disorder such that he does not even know whether it is physical or mental.[38]

The limits of anxiety-reducing practices are made abundantly clear if Levi-Strauss's claims of the organizational power of anxiety are accurate. If anxiety is merely mitigated when it becomes too overwhelming, then the way in which it is organizing reality will have been entirely skipped over. This is another weakness of the unconscious-overlooking behavioral models such as CBT, DBT and REBT. Through the aesthetically chess-styled mechanism described above, the therapist is immediately given access to how the client perceives interactions of the Other. "As the family, itself tends to change into a clan, the attribution of a different totem to each clan poses no problem."[39] The anthropologically studied idea of totemism is not simply a matter of dead history, but one which examines the organization of our psychical structure and fundamental understanding of the way in which reality is constructed.

It is important to keep in mind that the following is not a mandate for a rigorous systemic pathway forward to garner this type of information from clients, but a singular example of how a client with any belief system from any society can be shown the nature of power structures and how their relationship to them can be easily accessed. Once this relationship is accessed, a dialectic between the client's conscious and unconscious can be examined with the help of the therapist.

Let us journey to the beginning of this chapter where Žižek talks about the division of people into intellectual and manual workers and outcasts. It is a tempting idea for therapists to positively regard, as in the humanistic model, a client's complaints against someone in a different category from his. A reflection such as, "that must have been difficult," is standard fare and is considered an ethical response to a client describing an emotionally difficult event by, I would venture to say, nearly every practicing clinician in California. However, there is a better option. While a humanistic reflection acknowledging the client's difficulty is not to be disregarded, it does nothing to further the therapist's end goal of giving the client a working tool to process a similar situation in the future. How can the client come to understand and interact with people who inhabit materially different categories than them without slipping into the resentment of the Hysteric's Discourse?

Freud describes a two-part process which we can apply to the "incomplete" process of the behavioral models: "In acute stages of hysteria it will be necessary to await a calmer stage; in all cases where nervous exhaustion dominates the clinical picture a treatment which in itself demands effort, brings only slow improvement and for a time cannot consider the persistence of the symptoms, is to be avoided." This can be equated to the initial tools of the DBT or CBT therapist which are designed to relieve psychological tension and pain. Freud goes on to somewhat viciously write about people who, in his view, are not fit for analysis, "Furthermore, a certain measure of natural intelligence and ethical development may be required of him [the client]; with worthless persons, the physician soon loses the interest which makes it possible for him to enter profoundly into the mental life of the patient. Deep-rooted malformations...can scarcely be overcome."[40]

The traditional psychoanalyst fails this "worthless persons" patient in this case, utterly and completely. Believing that a client can only access their psychic lives by, essentially, having a level of insight comparable to that of Sigmund Freud, the founder of modern psychoanalysis, would be laughable if it didn't mean the marginalization of wide swaths of the population. It is akin to a physicist being angry that the average person cannot lie back on a couch and suddenly learn about the intricacies of quantum mechanics.

When the therapist shoulders the burden of implementing techniques that make the client's material position in terms of power dynamics apparent to them, the client can recover because the therapist in a humanistic manner abstractly "believes in them" as the truism goes, but also the patient will be able to understand why they are being subjugated. Once they understand why a seemingly negative force is intruding into their lives, they can adjust their relationship to it in a precise manner.

Chapter 6

The Liberated Subject

Yes of course there is a circle of life – but, the whole point is that there are different circles of life. A true revolution precisely is not an element of the circle of life – but it changes the very circle.
Slavoj Žižek, Signs from the Future [41]

It would be a mistake to presuppose that liberation refers to a vague notion of "freedom" from all methods of structural analysis. This primordial form of freedom should not deter us from a more refined, Lacanian definition of liberation. If one is doomed to various circles, then where does any sense of liberation come in? The answer is in the ability to change the very circle one is in, as Slavoj Žižek describes. Lacan explains in the Ecrits selection, "Beyond the Reality Principle," the nature of what Žižek describes as this circle of life, "The Freudian revolution, like any revolution, derives its meaning from context, that is, from the form of psychology that dominated at the time it occurred." [42] What does it mean that unconscious marginalizing therapeutic modalities in their various forms of neo-behaviorist cognitive treatments have come to signify the epitome of accurate assessment? It means that analysis that is not explainable in non-psychological common-sense terms is thrown to the wayside.

Common sense is simply not a valid measure of effectiveness in any context. The ease of pitching an idea that appeals to common sense is seductive, but nonetheless negates the nature of relativistic truth to essentially a dialectic between the unconscious and the conscious mind. What did it mean for holocaust victims that the common sense intuited by the German people was that the concentration camps were not up and running? Of course, it meant marginalization as valid human entities and death for prisoners in the concentration camp, but it also meant that the relativistic truth was that the concentration camp did not exist. At some unconscious level, the Germans believed that the Jews who were being taken away did not matter. Therefore, Lacan's idea of moving beyond the reality principle is so important when analyzing the material conditions of any contemporary field. It is not a denial of responsibility on the part of the person who recognizes relative conditions. It is, in fact, the opposite: willingness to take full responsibility for the implications of the falseness of the position as the-subject-supposed-to-know.

The seductive quality of stopping the work of psychotherapy at the reduction of negative symptomology cannot be underestimated. On anxiety, Cognitive Behavioral Therapy creator Aaron Beck writes, "When a person says 'I am nervous' he means that he is experiencing anxiety *right now*. But what does he mean when he says, 'I have a fear (or am afraid) of thunderstorms?' He is referring to a set of circumstances not currently present but that may occur sometime in the future."[43] One way a symptom can be reduced in a client who has such a fear of thunderstorms is to discuss with the client the irrational nature of fearing a thunderstorm that isn't in-the-now. The therapist can go over an algorithmic thought pattern, or a circle of thought, that involves deciding whether or not the fear is over something in the future that they can or cannot predict. Next, the therapist can ask the client if there is any reason to fear a thunderstorm. Sure, you can get hit by lightning, but that is highly unlikely. After these scenarios are processed with the client, the complaint of having a fear of thunderstorms can be reduced. This reduction is considered a success, and in a relativistic profession, it is impossible for me to refute that reducing fear is, in fact, a successful outcome. However, there is something missing.

What is a thunderstorm to the client? This is never examined except in the realm of conscious thoughts. It is highly likely, if not certain, that a phobia of thunderstorms is merely a signifier for another deeper aversion. This aversion could be due to many things. For example, a conflict that represents an attachment could have occurred during a thunderstorm, or this fear could be a metaphor that the client's unconscious constructs during the thunderstorm to extract a deeper meaning from the storm. Cloudy weather, rain and other weather events can be placeholders for deeper underlying issues. If I were having a problem dealing with interpersonal relationships and I went into the therapist's office to get my fear of thunderstorms under control, it is a perfectly reasonable capitalist notion that all that should be addressed in total is the fear of the thunderstorms. The client's symptoms are reduced as they wanted, and everyone is happy. The simplicity and straight-forward honesty of the cognitive model makes it extremely appealing.

This cognitive outlook, however, is unnecessarily short-sighted, because a therapist has the potential to provide the client with a savoir allowing the client to tackle problems in the future proactively. To what degree is it the job of the therapist to help the client become someone who can handle new problems, problems that have not even arisen yet? Is this not an imposition? Well yes, it is absolutely an imposition to suggest that the current cognitive circle of life needs to be overthrown, but that is the revolution that would allow for individuals who come into psychotherapy to get more than just symptom reduction, but instead a permanent change in their ability to deal with new events.

There has been a stagnation in the development of new psychodynamic theory because models are increasingly tailored to be easily explainable to people without any psychoeducation. The example of fear over thunderstorms is not muddy. Just because some lymphoma patients can be successfully treated with chemotherapy, that one treatment model does not negate the necessity for stem cell research. In other words, a model that works does not negate the necessity for an upgrade or an alternative model.

The upgrade from cognitive therapy would not be simply a movement backwards to Freud or a movement forward to Žižek. Instead, it would have to be both. Lacan writes in *The Ethics of Psychoanalysis*:

Is it to be found in a corner of Freud's work where one might overlook it, might consider it as merely contingent or even outmoded? I believe that everything in Freud's thought proves that that is by no means the case. And in the end Freud refers to this field as that around which the field of the pleasure principle is beyond the pleasure principle. Neither pleasure nor the organizing, unifying, erotic instincts of life suffice in any way to make of the living organism, of the necessities and needs of life, the center of psychic development...I don't want to indulge in overdramatization. All ages have thought they had reached the most extreme point of vision in a confrontation with something terminal, some extra-worldly force that threatened the world. But our absolute weapon that is waved in our faces in a way that is indeed worthy of the muses.[44]

A model of the psyche that only considers the client's wish to have a negative symptom reduced will be materially inaccurate due to the ignoring of what adds meaning to a human being's life. A human life is not simply one that avoids pain and runs toward pleasure. To engage in a practice of psychotherapy, whose material goal is to reduce one or more negative symptoms, is to do a disservice to the client because the therapist is, in fact, supposed to know. A client walking into a therapist's office is not someone who has necessarily gone to graduate school and is licensed to work in the field of psychotherapy. It is the job of the psychotherapist to determine the course of treatment.

Who is the psychotherapy client? If the person is there voluntarily, the psychotherapy client is someone who has come to a mental health professional because they believe they can obtain something from going to a mental health professional. If the psychotherapy client is in therapy involuntarily, it is even more important that the therapist, to whom the client's mental health condition has been entrusted, provides to the client the highest quality of care. The therapist may relieve a symptom of the involuntary client and then claim success, but again, this would be doing the client a disservice.

These are very grand sounding themes, but in fact, the actions required to implement these revolutionary words are all very small. To advocate for the new treatment model, psychotherapists must be able to demonstrate a working knowledge of their method to their fellow therapists, and make sense when describing them. As covered above in "How-to-Hegelese for the Everyday American," quoting Hegel to one's colleagues in a clinical environment where group decision is always the norm is not going to be effective because there needs to be a simply stated end goal.

The implementation of Lacan does not require a complex explanation of Lacan to a supervisor or one's colleagues. Lacan can be stated in common-sense terms that can be expressed in a clear manner that is understandable to insurance companies, which remains a requirement if the modality is to be accepted as valid. In addition, to be an ethical modality in a clinical setting, the method needs to be understandable and agreed upon by colleagues. While initially it may not seem like it, what is ethical *should* be determined by group acceptance; the reasoning is that adopted by California ethics law, where there is a distinct lack of central authority by design, for critical decisions to not be taken into the hands of a single therapist if the ideas of that therapist are ineffective. The new Žižekian angle to Lacanian psychotherapy is a method which allows therapists to communicate to other therapists the goals of their sessions with their clients in a clear, compelling manner.

The revolution in the field of psychotherapy will not begin with a bang, but must begin with a whisper. This is the only way a field that deals with the sensitive topic of mental health can change. It takes reasoned discussions with colleagues, supervisors, licensing authorities, insurance companies and all the other stakeholders in the field of mental health to move the ball forward. A single therapist has the power to effect hundreds if not thousands of people's lives in their professional capacity. With the number of people a single therapist can affect change upon, it is important that modern psychotherapy has advocates who understand that a therapeutic subject needs not only symptom reduction, but psychoeducation and a working algorithm to approach all the struggles faced in contemporary society.

Chapter 7

There is a Therapeutic Relationship

...the question that the schizophrenic's attitude poses for Freud, that is to say, the manifestly extraordinary prevalence of affinities between words in what one might call the schizophrenic world... The fundamental situation of repression is organized around a relationship of the subject to the signifier. As Freud emphasizes, it is only from that perspective that it is possible to speak in a precise, analytical sense – I would call it operational – of unconscious and conscious.

Jacques Lacan, The Ethics of Psychoanalysis[45]

The foundation of the therapeutic relationship must begin with the question, "Who exactly do you think you are?" This question should be posed from the client to the therapist. If this question is not directly asked by the client themselves, it is the therapist's job to inform the client of this question through various methods. One of the ways this key question can be invoked is for the therapist to simply ask the client, "What do you want out of therapy?" The client's answer to this question demonstrates who the therapist is seen to be by the client. In my practice, I have never heard a response, "To alleviate x symptom;" rather, the answer to this question is usually something along the lines of "I have x symptom." Other variations of this admission to the therapist resemble, "I am having x life problem" or, "In my relationship with my significant other, x is happening." A client's statement to the therapist that they want to alleviate a feeling is not equivalent to a client walking into the therapist's office because they have a symptom. There is a key difference between the two responses: "I want to alleviate x symptom" and "I have x symptom". The statement, "I have x symptom," is an unconscious question to the therapist, "What is to be done about this?"

Once again, the tenuous position of the therapist as subject-supposed-to-know is within the frame of reference. Who is the therapist, and why should they have any idea of how a client should move forward in any situation? It is especially important that a therapist has, if not a working knowledge of the Freudian unconscious, at least some notion of unconscious and conscious motivations. The signifiers a client presents are not a simple wish for a direct A to B process, but a wish for some sort of modification that is not yet fully known to the therapist or the client. The therapist, therefore, is not a subject-supposed-to-know as in the result, but instead is one who knows that there is a process of modification that the client seeks, that must be mutually determined through the signifiers presented in session. Lacan in the Ethics Lecture titled, "The death of God," asks "why in our everyday life do we find that in our metaphors a certain type of meaning is involved, certain signifiers that are marked by their primitive use with the sexual relation?...The metaphor used is employed to obtain a certain modification."[46] Not knowing may lead the therapist to a feeling of falseness with regard to structuring. Because the nature of signifiers is to constantly refer to other signifiers in a chain, the acknowledgment of a lack of immediately apparent truth or core can be seen as a nihilistic outlook. This would be the improper way to approach the use of signifiers, because the nature of signifiers reflects the true nature of perception. Signifiers which represent other signifiers. In Lacan's description of the sexual act, he describes the use of the signifier stating "...the principal actions in the making of a vase that I have previously emphasized, and something very precise, namely, not so much the sexual act as the female sexual organ." The slipping nature of signifiers makes itself obvious to the subject when it comes to sexuality because the neuroses around sexuality is, quite literally, felt by the subject. We must then, however, extrapolate these signifier exchanges, made apparent to us in the sexual relationship, to other relationships as well.

It is easy to see why some anti-analytical allies believe there is nothing to psychology and the unconscious, with a simple relativistic statement along the lines of, "No I did not mean anything except the thing that I said." However, it would be a mistake to assume that people ignore unconscious meaning simply because they do not believe that it is there. As Žižek writes in *First as Tragedy, then as Farce*, "like love, ideology is blind, even if the people caught up in it are not."[47] In other words, the choice of making the most easily insurance-covered modalities cognitive ones is not a choice based on the belief that the unconscious does not exist. Rather, it is a choice to mutually agree that the unconscious is not something that we prefer to investigate. With the Lacan-Žižekian outlook, one can unpack the true implication of the decision to simply act as if the unconscious is unreal. The unconscious seems as if it is something infinite, but in fact, the unconscious has a distinct character of slipping. While being unknown, it is not just a vast cavern of nothingness. The fear of the unknown depths of the unconscious can be looked at as a fear of the infinite number of possible interpretations of motivations and signifiers.

The unconscious itself has a distinct nature, and thus it is not an infinity, a depth to be lost in that is useless to investigate, but rather, the unconscious is a partial unknown. On Hegel's statement, "infinity is in itself the other of the being-other void," Alain Badiou writes, "The ontological impasse proper to Hegel is fundamentally centered in his holding that there is a being of the One; or more precisely, that *presentation generates structure*, that the pure multiple detains in itself the count-as-one."[48] Badiou goes on to brilliantly criticize Hegel's concept of an infinite void thusly:

Quantitative infinity is quantity qua quantity, the proliferator of Proliferation, which is to say, quite simply, the quality of quantity, the Quantitative such as discerned qualitatively from any other determination. But in my eyes this doesn't work. What exactly doesn't work? It's the Nomination. I have no quarrel with there being a qualitative essence Of quantity, but why name it 'infinity'? The name suits qualitative Infinity **because it was drawn from the void**, and the void was Clearly the transfinite polarity of the process...The radical absence Of the other, indifference, renders illegitimate here any declaration That the essence of finite number, its numericity, is infinite.[49]

The labeling of the unconscious mind as something infinite and unknowable is a mischaracterization of its quality as something which intrinsically carries with it descriptions of its contents as well. The unconscious in any analytical framework describes things which are repressed or unknown, but are nonetheless present in their absence. In the Freudian unconscious, specifically, the unconscious suggests a wealth of information that returns in a variety of forms, and is incapable of maintaining its absent nature. In speech, the repressed content returns in metaphor, metonymy and parapraxes (Freudian slips). In the non-verbal form, the unconscious content comes to the patient in a variety of symptomatic ways. **The symptom is not something which is simply a negative in the client's life; rather, the symptom is a way that the unconscious finds a means of expressing itself. It is in this expression that the symptom provides meaning.**

Repressed content returns as metaphor and as symptom; but also, information can be pushed on the client in the same manner of metaphor. When this happens, the client loses control of their ability to discern their needs or exactly the nature of "modification" that they are experiencing.

A typical establishing shot for a car commercial begins in

nature, on some curving mountain road, and then moves into the car, where the male from age 30 to 40 suddenly grips the wheel tighter and a small smile comes across his face. Then the back of the car is shown as it accelerates away. The crafty capitalist consumer, us, is totally unmoved by this. There is no way we will take up this ad on its offer that we spend tens of thousands of currency units on this vehicle because of the ad. But! When the analysis ends here, this is where we are swept up by the movement of ideology. Žižek writes, "The fear of the 'toxic' Other is thus the obverse (and the truth) of our empathy with the-other-reduced-to-a-fellow-man — but how did this syndrome arise?" Žižek further describes this toxic Other's power over us, "Instead of a hierarchical-centralized chain of command, we now see networks with a multitude of participants...capitalism is transformed and legitimized as an egalitarian project: accentuating auto-poetic interaction and spontaneous self-organization...."[50] When we say to ourselves, "I will not buy the car," we are nonetheless sold on the experience. Whether we buy a car from watching that ad, the experience as expressed to us, the consumer, in visual metaphor has been swallowed hook, line and sinker. "Sure," we may say to ourselves, "I am not going to buy this car, but isn't it freeing to just get in your car, and drive?" This car-driving enjoyment is relatively benign, but it's a mechanism of sale to us that must not go unexamined. When we recognize only the conscious singular message of "buy this car," we miss the underlying message of "this is how you will enjoy driving cars." Such advertising is repeated over and over and is targeted at fathers with minivans, and the working-class person who does no manual labor, rarely engages in outdoor recreation, but nevertheless insists on owning a pickup truck because that is the identity they feel belongs to them.When policy makers choose to ignore the unconscious, it makes painting over items that do not fit into a particular narrative that much easier.

In the name of capitalistic gain and clear communication,

therapy which only involves the conscious thoughts can be pitched to businesses and schools as a method to increase worker productivity or student academic improvement. A student's progress is measured based on their starting and finishing grade point averages. **The material analysis posed by the psychotherapy industry, which denies psychodynamic therapies that work with the client's unconscious, is not driven by a lack of belief in an unconscious. Rather, it is compelled by the commodifying of psychotherapy to the detriment of the psychotherapy patient.**

Slavoj Žižek describes in a chapter of *In Defense of Lost Causes* titled "Alain Badiou, Or The Violence of Subtraction," the following: "the traditional matrix of authority in which a community is established through sacrifice or is grounded in some primordial crime, so that it is guilt which keeps the members together and subordinates them to a leader."[51] What is subtracted when one denies the reality of the unconscious is anything which is predetermined by repression, which is something that is worth investigating. This is exactly the inverse of what psychotherapy methods should be. Repression is a necessary stepping stone in the process of psychotherapy, in that it determines what needs to be examined. When signifying chains are ignored, repression goes from being picked apart to being amplified and made the master of the psyche. What is repressed is the content that should be precisely uncovered, not deeply packed in.

The lost cause of the unconscious must be recognized not as an infinite void, but as having a material form that can be investigated and examined together with a clinician. When the unconscious is framed as an infinite void, it becomes something easily dismissed as esoteric and unknowable. The unconscious's contents are not necessarily completely accessible, but their nature as repressed content which is urgently relevant to current situations a client is facing, is known. To make it the therapist's duty to give the client the savoir to recognize their motives and the meanings of their actions is to provide a service to the client that a denial of the existence of such mechanisms cannot render. Furthermore, because the denial of unconscious mechanisms may be driven by the imperative of profit, it is not only a good idea, but the duty of any psychotherapist who claims to be working for the good of the client to advocate for methods most conducive to achieving a healthy, functioning and meaningful mental state. A belief that the sole duty of the therapist is to reduce symptoms misses the Žižekian vanishing point of the psychoeducated client.

Chapter 8

The Therapy Must Surpass Itself
{ø>1}->{1>ø}

*The Essence lights up **in itself** or is mere reflection: and therefore is only self-relation, not as immediate but as reflected. And that reflex relation is **self-Identity**. This Identity becomes an Identity, in form only, or of the understanding, be held hard and fast, quite aloof from difference... And this may be done in two ways. Either we may neglect a part of the multiple features which are found in the concrete thing (by what is called analysis) and select only one of them; or, neglecting their variety, we may concentrate the multiple characters into one.*
GWF Hegel, Logic[52]

Another way of writing the title for this chapter might be, "The client must surpass the therapist." This, however, is not entirely accurate, because in what must the client surpass the therapist, and where? The client must surpass the therapist's knowledge of the client themselves, which can be referred to as "The Therapy." The Therapy in this form, for the most part, must always start out in a place where the therapist is in the position of the-subject-supposed-to-know to some degree, and gradually the therapist becomes this less and less. Lacan writes of the destruction implicit in the creation of the narcissistic reflection of the subject:

In effect, it is quite certain that, if one begins from the notion of an original perfect narcissism in what concerns libidinal cathexis, if one conceives that everything which is of the subject in this narcissistic sphere, in this primitive monad of jouissance to which the baby is identified in a rather rash way, it is difficult to see what might be involved in a subjective escape from this primitive monadism. Now, if in this monad there is also included the devastating power of Thanatos, it is perhaps here that we can consider there to be the source of something which obliges the subject – if one can express it briefly in this way – to emerge from his self-envelopment.[53]

A destructive "Thanatic" drive is implicit at the outset of therapy. There is the wish of the client for the therapist to destroy something within them. In the Hegelian sense, this destruction can be an addition, because an additive property also negates the previous form of the client. Giving the client a simple tool for reducing negative feelings can fulfill the client's self-destroying wish for a movement in their initial being, and thus create the illusion of an ideal successful outcome. The jouissance in the client from their own self-destruction becomes a substitute for a deep algorithmic addition to their functioning. Because any addition which is also destructive by the very nature of its additive property is thus something which provides jouissance; precision is necessary in defining the outcome of the therapeutic process, even if the exact nature of this material outcome is unknown to both therapist and client. To presuppose a certain outcome resulting from a mere reduction in negative symptomology is a jouissance production in itself in the psychotherapist, whose simple goal is the subtraction of a negative property.

A matheme can be assigned to the therapeutic relationship and outcome goal, which would represent a success in giving the client an algorithmic mechanism that is more than just a coping tool, but instead a savoir or expertise in how to approach problems in their own subjective sphere. Because **the relationship in individual therapy consists of a therapist and a client, we can thus mathematically separate the binary therapeutic relationship of therapist and client in the following manner: the therapist can be assigned Zero/Void {ø} and the client can**

be assigned One {1}. The zero is a reference to the set theory void, but it is also similarly, a barred Other. The capital version of the void symbol (Ø)is sometimes used specifically in Lacanian theory in America to refer to the barred A, so ø will be used to symbolize the void of the therapist to avoid confusion to some degree.

In the beginning of the therapeutic process, the therapist is presupposed to have a working knowledge of the psyche, and is also assumed to have absolutely zero access to the client's internal world except via perceived phenomena. Hence the {ø} of the therapist comes to represent the lack of access the therapist has to the client's internal world. The client has neuroses, but the insight they have into their own neuroses can be seen as 'not enough,' since the client is in the office of the therapist. **Therefore, the beginning state of therapy can be represented as {ø>1}.** The therapist represents a narcissistic reflected excess of knowledge, comprised of an unknown field of knowledge which assists the client.

Žižek writes in his essay the following: "Bess' jouissance is a jouissance 'of the Other' in more than one way: it is not only an enjoyment in words but also (and this is ultimately just another aspect of the same thing) in the sense of utter alienation—her enjoyment is totally alienated/externalized in Jan as her Other." [54] In the same manner, the jouissance of the client in the initial phase of therapy lies in the perceived knowledge of the therapist as subject-supposed-to-know. There is the presence of an unknown {ø} which somehow knows. The therapist in this form takes on a sort of transcendental quality, which is not entirely unfounded, given the therapist's supposed ability to provide "movement" conducive to the client's well-being, without knowing anything about the client. The therapist possesses the savoir {ø>1} in the beginning. The therapeutic process should then aim toward {1>ø}, or the client surpassing this religious dimension of the therapeutic process and rising into a material expertise of themselves, which surpasses the therapist's ability to know the client.

It would be a mistake to believe that the transformative process of psychotherapy is done only through positive regard and building of the therapeutic relationship, because the therapist must assist the client in disregarding themselves and thus we are taken back to the field of jouissance, which includes within it its own destructive properties as well as healing properties. When the therapist provides the client with unconditional positive regard, the therapist remains a continued object of attachment, and thus the phase of {ø>1} is never fully transcended. In this non-psychoanalytical method, the jouissance of the client is always doomed to lie in the revering of the therapist as attachment figure.

Thus, it is the therapist's duty to have a client, who already possesses some form of the thing in itself in their own consciousness reflecting on their own consciousness, to have the endpoint of therapy reflect this possession. The therapist eventually gives up their hold as a partial religious figure to give the client back what they project into the therapist through transference at the beginning of the therapeutic process. Through psychoeducation and psychodynamic understanding of their own motivations, the client will undoubtedly come to recognize they possess the answer to their own questions, and need not rely on the knowledge of the Other to possess it. The beginning of the process {ø>1} thus transforms into {1>ø}.

{ø>1}->{1>ø} is a shorthand mathematical representation of the process of moving toward the Žižekian vanishing point.

The matheme of {ø>1}->{1>ø} has one more unexamined part, and that is the contents of the arrow. {->} is then The Therapy. This therapy must have certain formal qualities for the arrow to be a formally correct representation of the matheme {ø>1}->{1>ø}. One of the reasons that this book does not state that a specific modality is necessary for the client to obtain the greatest benefit from the clinical practice is that there are various methods by which to satisfy an algorithmic savoir. A clear distillation of Lacan is contained in *An introductory dictionary of Lacanian psychoanalysis:* "Lacan distinguishes between two kinds of knowledge: imaginary knowledge (*connaisance*) which is knowledge of the ego, and symbolic knowledge (*savoir*), which is the knowledge of the subject."[55] The problem with Cognitive Behavioral Therapy or DBT is that each only establishes a connaisance, an ego knowledge in the client, leaving unfulfilled the properties of The Therapy which establish the dialectic between the client and themselves. Marsha Linehan describes the goals of DBT as decreasing certain processes which are deemed harmful, such as mindlessness, conflict, non-flexibility, emotional instability, impulsive behaviors, and increasing positive skills such as mindfulness, interpersonal effectiveness, emotion regulation and distress tolerance.[56] There is nothing here which suggests a knowing of any sort of motivation outside of the initial conscious reactions to stimuli. The failing of this approach, which is based only on the ego self, is that it does not provide the client with the algorithmic savoir of themselves as subject to themselves. Thus, the therapist is always the holder of the expertise and the tools which the client uses to regulate their emotional state, and the therapy will always end $\{\emptyset > 1\}$-$>\{\emptyset > 1\}$. The therapist is the ultimate holder of expertise in the field because there is the agreed upon ideology to act as if there is nothing outside of conscious thought.

Algorithmic mathemes are not a means to transcend the detail of the therapeutic process through intellectual exercise. They are the Lacanian method of precisely inscribing into the therapeutic process the mechanisms which take place in his psychoanalytic method. Lacan writes on the notion of his algorithmic method of investigation into the subjective split of fantasy:

Of course, one may be surprised by the extent of what is

accessible to self-consciousness, on the condition that one has learnt it through another channel. Which is certainly the case here. For if we are to rediscover the pertinence of all this, a sufficiently sophisticated study, that can only be situated in the context of analytic experience, must enable us to complete the structure of fantasy by essentially linking here, regardless of its occasional elisions, the moment of a fading or eclipse of the subject – which is closely tied to the Spaltung or splitting he undergoes due to his subordination to the signifier...This is what is symbolized by the abbreviation ($<>A), which I have introduced as an algorithm; and it is no accident that it breaks the phonemic element constituted by the signifying unit right down to its literal atom. For it is designed to allow for a hundred and one different readings, a multiplicity that is acceptable as long as what is said remains grounded in its algebra. This algorithm and the analogs of it...are not transcendent signifiers; they are indices of an absolute signification, a notion which will, I hope, seem appropriate to the condition of fantasy without further commentary. [57]

Lacan's lecture on 'The Subversion of the Subject and the Dialectic of Desire' elicits the further necessity for us to take him seriously when he speaks of a dialectic of desire and an algorithmic signification. The reduction of the psychotherapeutic process to only ego content denies the client any insight into their own desire and their state as split beings. When the matheme {ø>1}->{1>ø} comes into play, the client is now at the point where they are beginning to be aware of the mechanisms of desire, and despite the state of admission to having less than total control of the mechanisms of their signifiers, the client can begin to understand in real time the nature of their existence and what is it exactly that should be done about it.

Chapter 9

Our Aggression, Our Castration, Our Fragmentation, Our Shit

A different series of relations (from penis envy) can be observed more distinctly in the male. It is formed when the boy's sexual curiosity leads him to discover the absence of a penis in women. He concludes that the penis must be a detachable part of the body, something analogous to fæces, the first bodily substance the child had to part with.
Sigmund Freud[58]

In *The Pervert's Guide to Ideology*, Slavoj Žižek explains to the viewer the significance of the plane graveyard. The graveyard is where once functioning planes are shown gutted and removed of their original significance as transportation vessels.[59] When the plane is gutted it is analogous to the earlier studied warm, flat Coca-Cola. When the Coca-Cola is robbed of its essential qualities, it has turned from the agent of enjoyment, into shit.[60] "These images of castration, emasculation, mutilation, dismemberment, dislocation, evisceration, devouring, and bursting open of the body—in short, the imagos that I personally have grouped together under the heading 'imagos of the fragmented body,' a heading that certainly seems to be structural."[61]

I do not wish to belay the finer biological assertions Freud makes regarding penis envy and the fear of castration, but there is an important truth in Freud's explanation of castration, the accuracy of which is more easily asserted. **The result of the subject's recognition of a quality or possession they possess, that has the descriptor of being "more" than an other, comes intrinsically linked with the fear of its removal. However, it is through this surplus that we are able to desire.** In other words, with a newfound ability or fortune comes the immediate suggestion that those things can be removed. With the penis, comes the suggestion of the removal of the penis. With good looks comes the suggestion of ugliness. With intelligence comes the fear of idiocy. With our family dinner comes the suggestion of waste and the starving children in Africa.

"It is evident ('a little *too* self-evident') that the letter has in effect, relations with location [le lieu] for which no French word has the entire import of the English adjective 'odd'...Language hands down its sentence to those who know how to hear it: through the use of the article employed as a partitive particle."[62] The signifier and its supposed meaning is only a fraction of its true implications. The recognition that it is more is only cut off due to a necessity of clarity. If this were only a matter of semantics, and there was no relation to the underlying neuroses of a patient, this reduction for the necessity of clarification would be all that was needed.

It is one thing to work through with a client the rationale of their fears. A person gets a promotion and suddenly is overwhelmed by anxiety. A therapist can listen to the client and work through what is and is not rational about fearing the new burden of the promotion. However, a client who knows that with the promotion comes the suggestion of the loss of the promotion, in the future can work through their relationship to risk on their own. It is like the ancient truism: give a man a fish and he eats for a day; teach a man to fish and he eats for a lifetime. If a singular symptom is a fish, then reducing symptoms resulting from such triggers as testing, heights, spiders and other fear-producing elements is giving the subject a fish. Teaching a client that a new positive thing in their life always comes with the suggestion of losing that thing enables the client to better understand their own mental processes as they are happening outside of the therapist's office. When a client has this ability, they can proactively engage with the surrounding world rather than being blindsided by anxiety, the mechanism of which they neither know nor understand. To understand the structure of the fear of the thing that provides enjoyment is to be able to better engage with things that involve enjoyment. A client who understands their own fears and motivations isn't necessarily someone who is more prepared to engage with challenges than a person who does not understand their own fears and motivations; however, a client who understands the mechanisms of their own fears should have a better chance than they would have without that understanding.

In *Lacan's Critique of the Ego Psychology*, Bruce Fink writes:

> It seems to me that Lacan's juxtaposition of the unconscious to the ego is an attempt to revitalize the debate and that his claim that this was in fact Freud's intent is a moot one, convincing as it may be in certain respects... Lacan perceived that this new obsession with the ego was so great that, although Anna Freud and the troika continued to pay lip service to other parts of Freud's theory—that is, although they occasionally say that their emphasis on the ego is **not** designed to invalidate interest in the id and the superego—in fact, they neglected the unconscious all together.[63]

There is an interesting rumor that I've heard from multiple sources, the full extent of its truth is uncertain, so if it doesn't work as fact, it at least works to illustrate a specific material point in the political process, and does a good job of acting as a narrative for our general psychic condition. This is the idea that the leader of North Korea is said, by official sources, never to defecate. This may or may not be Western propaganda, and the ambiguity works well here so I have refrained from Googling it, because it helps illustrate the relationship between anal retentiveness and malicious aggression. The figure of the North Korean leader as a cultural symbol in Western society is one of viciousness, controlling and spiteful. What would happen if the North Korean leader were to shit? What characteristic would be lost? With the title of Supreme Leader, part god, part king, comes the intrinsic quality of its disintegration. In other words, with the caviar comes the shit 12 hours later. There is no caviar without shit. In the same way, there is no narcissistic aggrandizement without the fear of the loss of such aggrandizement in the eyes of the Other.

If one were a psychotherapist for this fæcesless Dear Leader, what would one do? How could one come to terms with the aggression which partially manifests as the declaration that they do not defecate? It would be incorrect to call this assertion a type of psychosis, because culturally, he is never to defecate, or more accurately, state that he defecates. In a more realistic scenario, how is a therapist to approach a subject whose fear of the surplus value is linked with all their intrapsychic objects which they enjoy/desire?

The application of the theory has not been made entirely clear by Lacan, which is why a large part of this book attempts to outline the therapeutic process through client psychoeducation. Fink writes further in *Lacan to the Letter*:

> Those who have been reading Lacan for some time know how frustrating it can be to locate a particular thesis about, say, anxiety, and build on it and attempt to apply it clinically. Is this a neurotic strategy on Lacan's part: avoidance? Is he avoiding being pinned down because that would require him to take a stand, to put it all on the line with a particular thesis and argument, and thus expose himself to castration (that is, limitation, critique and the like)?[64]

For all the complaints about ego psychologists and cognitive therapists, there is one positive that can be acknowledged. The identification of the lack of an end goal of psychoanalysis has created a huge gap in the initial purpose of the entire endeavor. While there may be movement toward a greater functioning, there is a necessity to structurally express this movement. The matheme I suggest for the process of psychotherapy {ø>1}->{1>ø} is the movement toward that goal.

The ø in the formula that represents the lack of knowledge of the client-in-themselves, that the therapist represents from the client's perspective, has been used by Badiou in his theory of multiplicity to represent the void. The process of therapy is at heart a process for the function of the client, which is why the matheme {ø>1}->{1>ø} is written from the client's perspective, with the client as 1 representing their direct access to at least part of the thing in itself of themselves. The benefit that Lacan gives to the lecture hall, or that Žižek gives to the audience in his movies, is a movement toward this formula even if neither, due to their not being in a therapist/client relationship with the audience, fully fulfill the formula. If the viewer of the movie or the lecture is looking for the movie or lecture to provide some sort of knowledge in themselves, they fulfill the starting point of the position of The Therapy. The Therapy is represented as the arrow {->} in the matheme as the process in which a client goes from assuming knowledge in the void of the Other, from obtaining the structural knowledge of themselves, to algorithmically processing new events and situations in their own lives.

In an ironic twist, Žižek's view of himself not being taken seriously as a philosopher may be not only accurate, but directly caused by his function as the arrow {->} in the matheme. Žižek relays information to the general public about dialectic processing and psychoanalysis until the general public can interpret their own motivations and processing of information better than the void of the Other, Žižek himself.

The therapeutic agent's job is to render itself obsolete. Taking the proposal of having a psychoeducated client who is aware of the ways in which drive is manufactured through them in contemporary society, we may all be, in a sideways way, the client of this man who has no clients. In return, we provide the therapeutic agent with assertions that we know better than the agent does. We know better because a basic structural outline of the psyche is not as specific as our own individual psyches and the knots formed around our specific neuroses. The more we identify our chasing of surplus enjoyment, the enjoyment turning into shit, our fear of castration and various other mechanisms, the better we become at identifying the root causes of our symptomology that we term negative. The therapeutic agent becomes, if not obsolete, not completely necessary, and the client is set free from the process of psychotherapy. In other words, the therapist must give the subject the tools to dismantle their own house. The therapist must not hold onto the assertion that they are the subject-supposed-to-know who does, in fact, know. The therapist does not have access to the client's subjectivity-in-itself, only the client does. This is why the work to have the knowledge assumed from the void, aka {ø>1}, or the void of the therapeutic agent, is greater than the subject perceiving the void, eventually turns the corner through therapy, the arrow in the matheme ->{1>ø}, and the client becomes the expert on themselves in a way the Other never could. This is not to say the client will not lack knowledge in themselves that the therapist may have, but {ø>1}->{1>ø} is a good endpoint to keep in mind when in dialog with a client.

Chapter 10

Marriage for the Savvy Coca-Cola Drinker

The anal phase is defined by the adaptation of the subject's desire to the demand of the Other, i.e., the object-cause of the subject's desire (a) coincides with the other's demand...the oral phase does imply an attitude of wanting to "devour it all" and thus satisfy all needs... What then occurs in the anal phase is a dialectical reversal in this relationship between need and demand: the satisfaction of a need is subordinated to the demand of the Other, i.e., the subject (child) can only satisfy his need on condition that he thereby complies with the Other's demand.

Slavoj Žižek, Tarrying with the Negative: Kant, Hegel, and the Critique of Ideology[65]

With all the academic obsession surrounding Lacan's "there is no sexual relation" and Žižek's multitude of analyses on the subject, it's easy to forget the context in which this statement lives. While Žižek's joke about the ideal first date involving a dildo and a plastic vagina may seem to reduce sex to its basic components and half suggest that the role of sex is not as important as the symbol of sex, it obscures the nature of the genital organs themselves. Or as Žižek puts it, "And the function of the third, 'phallic phase,' of course, is precisely to disengage the subject from the enslavement of the demand of the Other."[66] What is the function of this seemingly pathological dialectic and how does it relate to relationship advice? Part of psychotherapy's ambiguity lies in its inability to be able to provide a single answer for an endpoint of psychotherapy. The matheme outlined earlier describes the knowledge that is to be delivered to the therapized subjects themselves, but it doesn't outline specifics of the therapy process for every patient because it cannot function in that manner.

What would a psychoanalytically healthy marriage look like? Much in the same way the Borromean Knot ties together the Lacanian orders of the Real, Imaginary and Symbolic, much of psychoanalytic work can be described as a way of moving around the neuroses from a register in which it is stuck. Someone who has a fixation with something that is rooted in the thinking of symbolic order can be aided by a therapist helping the client provide an imaginary context, and to some degree, exposing the therapeutic subject to their own emotions regarding the up-close relationship to the root cause of the complaint, or exposure to the Real. Lacan writes on his theory of knots:

> We do not believe in the object, but we observe desire. From this observation of desire we infer that the cause is objectal [objectivée]. The desire for knowledge encounters obstacles. As an embodiment of this obstacle I have invented the knot. The knot must come undone. The knot is the only support conceivable for a relation between something and something else. If on one hand the knot is abstract, it must at the same time be conceived as concrete. This American ordeal, which is the reason I'm so weary today, has certainly been worthwhile, because I was able with these diagrams to create some agitation, some emotion. The sensed as mental, the senti-mental, is idiotic, because always by some device reducible to the imaginary. The imagination of consistence immediately extends to the impossibility of rupture [cassure], but it is in this that rupture can always be the real, the real as impossible, which is no less compatible with the said imagination, and even constitutes it…the knot which may be termed borromean cannot be cut without dissolving the myth it offers….[67]

What is the role of this myth the knot offers and why does

the knot of the myth need to be undone in psychotherapy? In a relationship, the knot is the myth surrounding the supposed subject of the Other. The three primary stages of Freudian development really get to shine in the relationship setting, especially in relationships with some pathology, either conscious or unconscious. First, there is the need to consume all, fulfilled by the oral neuroses. Then, the need to tidy up, fulfill the demand of the partner or the relationship-in-itself (a Big Other). Then, there is individuation. The phallic aspect of the relationship. The latent and genital stages of the relationship are somewhat irrelevant for this particular knot, the latent stage involving lack of sex and the genital stage being a symbol for maturity. While this describes a human's transition into adulthood, Freud's initial stages are the perfect rings in which to examine the symptomatology of the relationship. **For Lacan, the subject does not exist, and it is in the knotting that the nature of the illusion of the subject reveals itself. The need to untie the knot and show its components to the analysand in Lacan's world is as close to a concrete goal as one may find in Lacan's writing on sinthome.** *The therapized subject gives too much, wants more, wants to individuate or experiences all three of these things in a relationship. Through Lacan's method of the knot and Žižek's contemporary analysis of desire, the knot of the Coca-Cola savvy marriage subjects begins to become discernible through its untying.*

It is interesting that the phrase, "to tie the knot," is another way of stating one's moment of marriage. What is being tied together here? It is libidinal energy, neurosis, the combining of subjective beings who are threatened with dissolution as the surplus value reveals itself as having an intangible quality; these things are tied into the marriage. The marriage becomes a symptom, or in this case because it is a specifically Lacanian concept dealing with knots, sinthome.

The relationship with the knot is caught up in what can be

called a Binary of the Will. Lacan writes, "I am trying to give you a bit of real, concerning this in which, in the skin of which, we exist – in other words the skin of that implausible history, the human species. And I say to you that there is no sexual relation." Lacan continues, "But it's embroidery. It is embroidery because I take part in 'yes or no'. From the moment I say there is no, I, it is already very likely not to be truly a bit of real, because the cicatrice of the real is that it is linked to nothing."[68] If there is no sexual relation, and the cicatrice (scar) left by trauma is not linked to the symbolic order, then what exactly is Lacan saying yes or no to? There is an embroidery created with the batteries of signifiers in a relationship. These in relational terms can be looked at as various interactions between the partners, a give and take model. The oral partner takes, the anal gives, and both individuate through the phallic regression and question it all. However, the idea that because of this, one should never engage in a relationship or a marriage at all is putting the cart before the horse. Just because deconstruction of a situation reveals the gritty detail does not mean it is here where one should disengage and retreat into a world where one never pokes holes through the trauma of the real. It doesn't mean that because one person takes that the other person who is tired of giving, or wishes to individuate, should simply regress from the scene all together. Yet the neuroses of a relationship and the economy of desire are pulled by these unconscious possibilities, this lack in the embroidery if you will.

The savvy Coca-Cola drinker knows that the surplus value they experience while drinking the Coca-Cola has a nature of emptiness to it, but nonetheless they drink it. It is not necessary for Coca-Cola to have a specific material quality for someone to drink a Coca-Cola; there only needs to be an embroidery which renders the object as something which contains an element that is more than the sum of its parts. Within the disconnect, there is meaning to be had and desire to be integrated more fully into the life conducive with values and personality. Fink writes:

> According to Saussure, the signifier and the signified, the sound-image (or sound pattern) and the concept, are indissolubly tied together...This is an encapsulated sign, a sign in which the signifier and signified do not seem to slip away from each other, forming instead a yin-yang-like configuration. Lacan unceremoniously abolishes the enclosure, eliminating the apparent harmony of the image and the seeming totality it forms.[69]

At first glance it may be difficult to ascertain the advantage of taking such a view on the nature of signifiers, especially when acknowledgment of the intrinsic lack in a relationship's signifying chains carries with it the hint of a seemingly negative aspect to understanding. Immediately to the psychoanalytically attuned reader, the idea of unpacking as a negative will stand out as a mechanism of repression of content. One need not analyze a relationship and unpack every single knot, but when a relationship comes to the phase where it is brought up in the therapy session, the knots must be untied and examined.

The untying will bring with it the essentially analytic movement of any process which moves toward the therapy subject becoming more aware of the nature of how their desire interacts with the rest of their psyche. Lacan's idea of the power of desire to curve the space of perception alongside Lacan's theory of knots leads to a two-fold realization. One, that the psychoeducation process must always examine the mechanisms of desire, and two, that the psychoeducation process is a confronting of things that are tied off, or emotionally repressed for the sake of ordering. A melancholic disposition may take over the subject who cannot understand the mechanisms of their desire, nor the ways in which they are cut off from the understanding of their patterns of desire, due to the inability to untangle the knot and examine its contents.

Relationship dynamics are always going to be undefinable, out of reach. One notices that it fluctuates. "Is not every speech-act the coup de force of a particular unconscious, a collectivization of the unconscious?" Lacan asks. "If every speech-act is the coup de force of a particular unconscious, it is quite clear that every speech-act can hope to say something, and this saying gives onto something theorized, theory being the support of all kinds of revolution – a theory of contradiction."[70] The relationship between two individuals, or perhaps more, even in the case when there are only two in the sexual relationship, is one of knots. Perhaps at its best, a relationship is much like the now archaic sail-based warship titans; a constant tying off and unraveling, tying off and unraveling, to a direction that is determined by the dynamic ocean.

Chapter 11

Mental Health, an Industry of Knots

Today's basic productive force is thus the "cognitariat," the multitude of cognitive workers; their work produces freedom, and their freedom is productive.
Slavoj Žižek, In Defense of Lost Causes[71]

It would be a mistake to look at therapists as simple petty bourgeois exploiters who, through greed, have failed their patients. The fact of the matter is that there are knots around the cognitive dissonance where capitalism and mental health efficacy intersect. To tie together patient care, supposed affordable pricing and both private and public insurance involvement, the symptom or dissonance in the modern therapy industry is tied in a knot around cognitive modalities that can be explained step by step, with as many statistics as possible that prove the method works. We psychotherapist cognitariat workers are then left in the position of tying knots that hide the lack intrinsic in the profession itself, the main subject of which is the abstract and confusing plane of the mind. "The ego is a thing which I've been thinking about with a knot...But supposing, says Milnor, you allow that in any chain, a particular element can traverse itself, you will then have this, which immediately shows you that what went under here, in the center, foes over there – there is no longer a knot, a link."[72]

The forcing of pragmatism onto the psyche ties a knot to relieve the mental health industry of its symptomatic anxiety. "In sum, psychoanalysis is an example, nothing more, of a short-circuit which passes through meaning...the compilation of language (as it is with this that I support the unconscious) with our bodies."[73] This is too much for an insurance claim, and so a reductionist viewpoint for simplicity's sake is created. The unconscious is considered when it will not make too many waves, or when it fits in nicely with some other cognitive model. For therapists to constantly deal with the ambiguity of the unconscious, requires not taking a position that insists on lack being disintegrated. In other words, it takes a discourse that is willing to not know fully an answer. This doesn't work in contemporary society that relies on capitalism to determine the most effective treatments, so a knot is formed to stifle the anxiety surrounding the ambiguous nature of a psyche. A therapist is looked at much in the same way as any trades person would be looked at. This has benefits. Quacks get weeded out; people cannot just give advice to patients and call themselves therapists; people who set up celebrity rehab centers and then break confidentiality to the press get their licenses revoked, and thus therapists are regulated. In the medical profession, there is a necessity for accountability. This is where the issue becomes difficult to contend with. What does it mean that one does not necessarily know what the outcome of the treatment will be from the start, because one does not know the stories and signifiers that the client will provide when they walk into the room? Furthermore, how can one possibly express that a client having symptoms reduced in psychotherapy isn't a great success? In many ways, it is a success to have a client walk into an office in emotional distress, and walk out in less emotional distress due to the talking cure providing a space to "chimney sweep," as the first talking cure patient put it.

There may not be an alternative to tying these knots. We can examine the knots which allow the mental health field to function through the lens of capitalism, but there is much room to improve this model. If the treatment plan is effectively determined by what gets funding or not, one is completely reliant on the free market and profit to decide a remarkably large amount of what works and what does not work. This is different than the traditional medical model where one has a physical ailment and there is not much wiggle room to decide whether or not the treatment was effective. However, in mental health treatment, the end position of therapy is determined by a philosophy. There is no objectively correct answer to when therapy should begin, how it should proceed or how it should end. The DSM attempts to classify various traits in groupings, so one can get a picture of how a patient should be diagnosed, based on how many symptoms one is experiencing, which maximally overlap with one or more of the disorders listed.

Patient care is intricately linked with these knots in economic functionality and form of treatment. The treatment form's foundation is built on the economic reality of the licensing area and the client's socio-economic status. However, there is also the knot formed between the imaginary register projection that the patient has of the therapist and the symbolic ordering of treatment modalities. Because there is always an assumed knowledge that the therapist can help the client in some way that the client is unable to help themselves with, there is a faith in the therapist to have insight, but that insight is intangible.

This indiscernibility works to the therapist's benefit in many ways. It gives them flexibility, and it allows the therapist to use clinical judgment. But this structure requires the therapist to be the holder of responsibility for the client's outcome. With this much faith in the ability of the therapist, the therapist should not only provide to provide a good outcome, but should also help determine what constitutes a good outcome, and the therapeutic ethical code should reflect back onto the therapist the responsibility for the outcomes of their works. The ethical code protects both therapist and client, so it is very important how the ethics code, the therapist and the client all determine what is the outcome of treatment.

This goes back to the main purpose of the text, which is to propose that there needs to be a fundamental shift in how we ascertain therapeutic efficacy. There needs to be more than just a reduction of symptoms, because the reducing of a negative does not suggest a positive. In less Western, amorphous, pseudo-intellectual terms, there needs to be provided a path forward. The path forward that should be added to the standard of practice can only be achieved with psychoeducation; and specifically, the way in which new desire is manufactured in the client in relation to the initial reason for being in the therapist's office.

To suggest that we look to the past, to Freud and Lacan, in order to find a new ethical code may seem counterintuitive, but when capital reterritorializes the psyche into systems based on their compatibility with viral market shares of the mental health topographical map, it is hard to argue for an ever-forward, arc of history that always bends toward justice. This is where ethics must come into play.

> Ethics is not simply concerned with the fact that there are obligations, that there is a bond that binds, orders, and makes the social law. There is also something we have frequently referred to...(as) 'the elementary structures of kinship' – the elementary structures of property and of the exchange of goods as well. And it is as a result of these structures that man transforms himself into a sign, unit, or object of a regulated exchange....[74]

Lacan, and specifically the Žižekian method of material analysis, does not consider it good enough that there is a circle of life that happens to function systemically. The system needs to fundamentally be altered so that patient care and successful outcomes are prioritized.

There are two major ethical terms when it comes to proper ethical technique. Leaving aside the ways in which therapy becomes completely useless (there are a million ways to skin a cat, for example), which is beyond the subject of this book, the first is standard of care, and the second is best practice. To be up to the standard of care means that if one were to present the treatment of a client to another therapist, the paperwork ducks would be in a row, the method of treatment would have reasoning behind it that is comprehensible and goal-oriented, and the outcome generally would not be put on the shoulders of the therapist. I am not stating that, ethically, the blame should be shifted to the therapist even if the therapist followed a modality to the letter; the therapist should be held responsible for a patient who, in their self-assessment, did not benefit from therapy.

There is something morbid in the idea that one should revolt in a realm such as psychotherapy, in that there is a suggestion of a fundamental negation of the current mental health industry. "The dialectical relationship between desire and the Law causes our desire to flare up only in relation to the Law, through which it becomes the desire for death. It is only because of the Law that sin…takes on an excessive, hyperbolic character," states Lacan.[75] **The reason that a signifier such as revolt is so necessary and apropos in this situation is that the vanishing point proposed is one that gives efficacy into the hands of the patient. The revolution that this book suggests is not one of negating through subtraction of coping techniques, but a negation of Band-Aid therapy through the addition of a psychoeducational model within a variety of already existing approaches.**

The Žižekian vanishing point is not the same as the Lacanian ideal which, at its roots, is a long form therapeutic process investigating the nature of the client's knots. This can still be done with Žižekian psychoeducational aspects, but the Žižekian vanishing point is more so a challenge to the cognitive models that claim to reduce the complexity of the psyche because there simply isn't enough time to investigate the nature of the psyche. It doesn't take a year to have signifiers be brought up multiple times by clients, or to return consistently throughout sessions. These signifiers are points which are knots. These knots can be expanded upon, and it isn't a matter of being able to make wild

Freudian interpretations, but simply a matter of recognizing that there is a linguistic method of analysis in a client's story. Words and themes that return on the Moebius Strip are methods of controlling various emotional suppressions. Rather than the melancholic fixating on the things that are upsetting them, there is a repression and suppression for fear of the letter arriving at the destination where it already is. The depressed patient fears being depressed, but they are already oppressed. This fear leads them to tie knots to prevent a condition from which they are already suffering.

It does not take an analytical genius to look for the repeated signifiers for various stressors and points of meaning. The expression of the melancholic is the pulling apart and examining the nature of the knot, and the beginning of a way forward for the client. This, rather than simply offering coping mechanisms for anxiety, should be recognized as best practice, ethically speaking, because it not only reduces symptoms, but it provides the client with the template to reduce symptomatology in the future without the therapist's presence.

Chapter 12

Intrapsychic Liberalism's Sunset, Also Batman

Such is the fright that seizes man when he discovers the true face of his power that he turns away from it in the very act—which is his act—of laying it bare. This is true in psychoanalysis. Freud's Promethean discovery was such an act, as his work attests; but that act is no less present in each psychoanalytic experience humbly conducted by any one of the workers in his school.
Jacques Lacan, Ecrits [76]

The power of Freud's Promethean discovery (the Olympian fire brought down to earth for the use of mankind) relies on the assessment and material application of conditions which lie underneath the surface of ruling discourse. For Freud this is the unconscious subverting the conscious; for Marx it's material analysis of the human cost of the petty bourgeoisie's use of value exchange to further their value accumulation. Insofar as Žižek has done the important work of noting how freedom has become synonymous with vulgarity in the Trump era, the signifier of liberalism may be doomed due to the inevitable erosion of a signifier based on its ability to never assert its own accuracy via force. Or rather, that force is always submerged to the unconscious of those who have a totemic hold on freedom as public policy, via the application of force in a liberal (in the classical sense), capitalist society. In other words, Žižek seems to have found his task in doing the analytic work for the abstraction of capitalism as a whole, as he points out in his analytic fashion the current material conditions of various dissonances and symptoms in various states of the Imaginary, Symbolic and Real triad.

We should not underestimate Žižek's ability to point out where society has tied a knot to alleviate its dissonance, creating the sinthome which has strings that need to be untied and examined. In a proper Lacanian therapy, if the client's psychic economy is pushed by impulse toward a non-existent freedom from all signifying chains leading to a psychotic-styled distress, there is a necessity for them to begin to link signifiers together in a manner that allows them to function properly in the world of language and symbols; that is to say, the client should become integrated into a symbolic order. Thus, the analytic process works from an individual level to an international systemic level. Lacan writes on the subject:

> The concept of libidinal object relations which, by renewing the idea of treatment progress, is quietly altering the way treatment is conducted. The new perspective began here with the extension of psychoanalytic method to the psychoses and with the momentary receptiveness of psychoanalytic technique to data based on a different principle... a clear-cut reaction is working in favor of a return to symbolization as the crux of technique.[77]

The recognition of the batteries of signifiers is one thing, but the morphing of them into a chain which provides the client with their own psychical savoir relating to their intrapsychic mechanisms outside of the therapeutic process involves a series of sessions. It is important to not let the fact that one session is not enough go unanalyzed. Why is it that we must go through a series of therapeutic sessions to get a benefit from psychotherapy? If they just need insight into their own psychic condition, could not a talented therapist assess the mechanisms of the neuroses and deliver the client the message of their mechanisms and what they need to do differently? The reason is the complexity of the signifying chain is tied in with the unconscious nature of batteries of signifiers, many of which the client has displaced outside of their own conceptual self.

> The analyst leaves room for this Other beyond the other by the neutrality with which he makes himself be ne-uter, neither the one nor the other of the two who are there; and if he remains silent, it is in Order to let this Other speak. The unconscious is the Other's discourse in which the subject receives his own forgotten message in the inverted form suitable for promises.[78]

The temporality of the analytic process should not be ignored. There is a time period required for the movement of signal shifts in the signifier battery. The message of the subject of therapy has knots that are not only invested in their own definitions of self, but are in a Lacanian sense tied up in the Other as well. Thus to tell somebody something they don't know about the information which they are giving regarding themselves is to give them information which is specifically abjected from themselves and tangled in the Other.

The therapeutic process is not a simple relaying of information regarding certain signifiers, but a process of shifting those signifying chains. Žižek writes on the complex relationship between the signifiers placed in the self and the various forms of the Other:

> ...the dead son who appears to the father with the terrible appeal, 'father, can't you see that I'm burning?', Lacan's statement can also be paraphrased as the reproach to the God-Father: 'Father, can't you see that you're dead?'[79]

The Other takes many forms: a father, a god, a villain, a hero, and thus signifiers and fantasies are tangled up in a web of not only one's own belief about themselves, but about the world around them which is inevitably filtered through the perceptive lens of the therapeutic subject, and is in some form a part of the therapeutic subject, even if abjected into the Other. Narratives which are not related back to the Moi identity contain clues regarding the contents of the psychic condition. The psychic condition is not only about how people relate to themselves and their immediate conditions, but also about the narratives projected into the Other. Or as Žižek puts it in regards to the cured patient who no longer thinks he is grain but is none-the less worried about being eaten by the chicken, "Therein resides the true stake of psychoanalytic treatment: it is not enough to convince the patient about the unconscious truth of his symptoms, the unconscious itself must be brought to assume this truth."[80]

The necessity of creating the unconscious links in order to deal with underlying neurosis is done in session with a dialectical exchange between the client/therapeutic subject and the therapist/analytic agent. The capitalist method of assessing the patient who believed themselves to be a piece of grain would not have been able to account for the underlying condition. Having then not created a savoir allowing for a working algorithm with which to approach new stimuli and new or returning motifs, the client is failed by the mental health system. For the therapist to state that the client is treated due to the fact that they are saying "I am no longer dealing with the conscious chief complaint" is to alleviate the therapist of the responsibility of having expertise regarding the nature of the psyche. Much in the same way that democratic capitalist societies state that their system is best because when there is no king, there can be no tyrant, the mental health system states that because the objective measurements of cognitive interventions are the measure of success, no therapist can screw up by making an interpretation, because psychodynamic therapists rely on interpreting symbols and obviously, something can be misinterpreted.

The policy of intrapsychic liberalism can be summed up in the total de-pathologizing approach to being a therapist. It isn't a problem unless the client says it is a problem because there are many different ways to live. The issue with this live and let live approach is that it puts no responsibility on the therapist to provide the client with a structural framework for moving forward. Humanistic approaches can reflect onto the client attachment which they never experienced from an authority figure before, but what does the client do after they are done being unconditionally positively regarded?

The humanistic approach may in fact work when they unconsciously link signifiers, but this is akin to the Žižek assessed policy of the new Batman films where people are protected through systemic lying. [81] When the truth is claimed to be not enough, what sort of method the citizens of Gotham have to protect themselves from future malicious intentions from real existential threats to themselves is not the main issue; the Other of the state can no longer protect the information repressed to the political unconscious which is too damaging for the state actors to function at its reveal. Whether or not there is a crime serious enough for the state of democratic capitalism itself to collapse is unlikely, but in the Gotham city state, it is made clear that this would lead to anarchy in the form of the villainous ideologies coming to power. The proletariat of Gotham is thus deprived of agency in the name of humanistic goodwill, but this in itself is not necessarily the problem; the problem is that in this scenario, passivity and freedom are based off of the repression of the unconscious content which states to the citizenry to never know its composition, the information which suddenly can pop up and collapse the whole thing.

Unlike in a Stalinist system where information such as "you know, there are gulags as well," somehow being leaked to the public would not be new or surprising information, the scenario of Batman as the holder of truth becomes a powderkeg for the return of the repressed to collapse the entire Gotham city-state structure.

Žižek states regarding the structure of a functioning Other, "... interpassivity is the opposite of Hegel's notion *List der Vernunft* (cunning of Reason), where *I am active through the Other*: I can remain passive, sitting comfortably in the background, while the Other does it for me." [82] The role of the Other is a fundamental lynch pin for the entire structure of the therapeutic process. Let's assume for a minute that the therapist is The Batman also known as the Dark Knight (and there are a lot of symbolic parallels to be drawn between the idea of the therapist who functions as the agent that can see into the darkness of the unconscious and The Batman whose function is to operate in the unconscious of the social order). What becomes the function of the agent that works in the darkness of the unconscious? When in *The Dark Knight Trilogy* Batman makes the decision to take the fall for the societal symbol Harvey Dent's great crimes but with this comes the making of the Dark Knight, the ethical agent working with the unconscious content, essentially creating a master signifier of untruth. Thus, the societal unconscious will never be healed, and the social being knows they are not grain, "but does the chicken know it?" The symptom is then not dealt with because the unconscious itself does not take hold of the cognitive dissonance between values and the actions of power, but relies on a total schism between the conscious subject of the Gotham citizen and the unconscious therapeutic agent of Batman.

What exactly would have been the consequence of allowing society to know that Harvey Dent was a killer, someone who experienced trauma then began to commit morally reprehensible acts? What was the Dark Knight trying to save society from? The therapeutic agent no longer works for society when it denies the unconscious content's necessity; the therapeutic agent only morphs into something which acts as a further mechanism of repression, causing future returns of the repressed to become violent. This is not an argument for the revelation of all state secrets per se, but rather for the internal state secret agents of actions to not lie to themselves about the significance of the individual signifiers which they are in possession of. The Dark Knight, the ethical therapeutic agent, must know the functioning of itself in a material. **The therapist in the clinic must not project their discomfort for unconscious content into the work and avoid it for the sake of the therapist's own discomfort for working with volatile materials.** When this happens, it is inevitable after the Joker leaves, Bane is right behind, ready to return the unconscious content back to the conscious violently.

Chapter 13

Voodoo Child Subject (Slight Return to Hegel)

Well, I stand up next to a mountain,
and chop it down with the edge of my hand
Well, I pick up all the pieces and make an island
Might even raise just a little sand
Jimi Hendrix, Voodoo Child (Slight Return)

Neurosis is understood via the client's neurotic symptoms being acted out in the room, thus to simply give the client tools to reduce their feelings that they deem uncomfortable is not enough to understand the root causes. As Lacan states:

To return psychoanalysis to a veridical path, it is worth recalling that analysis managed to go so far in the revelation of man's desires only by following, in the veins of neurosis and the marginal subjectivity of the individual, the structure proper to a desire that thus proves to model it at an unexpected depth—namely, the desire to have his desire recognized.[83]

This is not to say coping tools are unnecessary, and when a psychotherapist has a client in great psychic distress and the psychotherapist is able to somewhat stabilize the client through a tool such as mindfulness or some sort of cognitive rational, the psychotherapist finds themselves grateful for that end of mental health. However, this is not the treatment; rather, this is the precondition for the beginning of the work of therapy in the same way one cannot work on a car engine unless the engine is off. They can look into themselves and get somewhat of an understanding of the mechanisms of desire, but it is through the analytic process with the Other who presents their free-associative thoughts that neurosis was mapped and that Freud and Lacan made their discoveries about the human psyche. Partly of course they examined themselves, but all theories were only good insofar as they were observed in the client, and able to be applied via psychoanalysis. The analyst functions as a conduit, although not a total blank slate, to the therapeutic subject's unconscious. Lacan writes of this:

> Presence of the analyst—a fine phrase that should not be reduced to the tear-jerking sermonizing, the serous inflation, the rather sticky caress to be found in a book that has appeared under this title. The presence of the analyst is itself a manifestation of the unconscious, so that when it is manifested nowadays in certain encounters, as a refusal of the unconscious—this is a tendency, readily admitted, in some people's thinking—this very fact must be integrated into the concept of the unconscious. You have rapid access here to the formulation, which I have placed in the forefront, of a movement of the subject that opens up only to close again in a certain temporal pulsation—a pulsation I regard as being more radical than the insertion in the signifier that no doubt motivates it, but is not primary to it at the level of essence, since I have been driven to speak of essence.[84]

There is a certain relationship that the therapist and the therapeutic subject must have which provides the therapeutic subject with insight into essence through the medium of speech, since psychoanalysis and psychotherapy, barring some art therapies and kinetic therapies, are mostly based in speech. "The unconscious is the sum of the effects of speech on a subject, at the level at which the subject constitutes himself out of the effects of the signifier."[85] Speech itself is a subversive act that transcends the subject's simple thoughts. The ego in the subject can be formed in a vacuum without speech, somewhat. There is no relinquishing of meaning in conversation with a subject when one exists without speech.

The aspect of being the therapeutic subject or the client in itself allows for one to experience the therapeutic process, which is a dialectic formed at the locus of the split subject of the client. The client must always return to their castrated-state of becoming split and reduced by language in order to engage in the therapeutic process which can untie the knot and examine the contents of the neurosis. Žižek's especially Hegelian reading of Lacan connects Hegel and Lacan's joint relation to the client's speech:

> Hegel was right to point out again and again that when one talks, one always dwells in the universal—which means that, with its entry into language, the subject loses its roots in the concrete life world. To put it in more pathetic terms, the moment I start to talk, I am no longer the sensually concrete I, since I am caught up in an impersonal mechanism which always makes me say something different from what I wanted to say—as the early Lacan liked to say, I am not speaking, I am being spoken by language. This is one way to understand what Lacan called "symbolic castration": the price the subject pays for its "transubstantiation" from being the agent of a direct animal vitality to being a speaking subject whose identity is kept apart from the direct vitality of passions.[86]

If our vitality comes from our passions, what is the relation that speech has as a force which vitality itself does not have? The therapeutic process is rightly questioned based on the fact that the analyst themselves has a high degree of determinacy of the process of therapy itself. This leaves a lot of room for various techniques both legitimate and quackery such as the Orgone accumulation box.[87] This is why the early expressed matheme {ø>1}->{1>ø} was proposed to represent the client engaging in a therapeutic process which leads them to understand the way their own desire shapes their world. The arrow represents The Therapy, which can include speech which leads the client to understand the nature of their desire.

If the client is the one who castrates themselves via speech cutting down their ego due to the lack intrinsic in the explanations for their various internal states and observed phenomena, then what is the therapist's role but to propagate this castration? Desire makes itself apparent and thus the roots of the client's issues based on the signifiers is presented in the analytic process. As the signifiers begin to reveal a common connecting theme, the therapist continues the process by noting common connecting factors. A grouping of themes relating to animals can be noted, or a theme relating to conflict between family members.

Žižek's specifically Hegelian approach to Lacan can be useful in that the process can continue when keeping in mind the Žižekian vanishing point of the psychoeducated client represented by the {ø>1}->{1>ø} matheme. Žižek's view of Hegel can be used to show the important difference between a Žižekian vanishing point of the therapeutic process and a purely Lacanian or Freudian one. Žižek writes on the topic of reason:

> Hegel's crucial step towards maturity occurs when he really "abandons the paradigm of the polis" by reconceptualizing the role of civil society. First, civil society is for Hegel the "state of Understanding," the state reduced to the police-apparatus regulating the chaotic interaction of individuals each of whom pursues his egotistic interests. This individualistic-atomistic notion of freedom and the notion of a legal order imposed on individuals as an external limitation of that freedom are strictly correlative. The need thus arises to pass from this "state of Understanding" to the true "state of Reason," in which individuals' subjective dispositions are harmonized

with the social Whole, in which individuals recognize the social substance as their own.[88]

Žižek's view of the world is more structured than Lacan's view of constantly slipping signifiers in that the agency of knowledge or the University Discourse is consciously allowed to play some role even though it may lack in a psychoanalytic sense, the agency of the truth it claims to hold. In psychotherapeutic practice, this uniquely Hegelian reading of Lacan allows for a new possibility in outcome that was not emphasized in the Lacanian approach of Freudian psychoanalysis which unpacks signifiers and examines the contents of knots. Hegel's concept of a State of Reason can be said to be an endpoint that is based on the State of Understanding, which can be seen as the traditional goal of psychoanalysis. The desire which is recognized with the integration of this perverse Hegelian addition to Lacan's discourse is the desire for a savoir like the therapist's, and the cutting tools that come with such an expertise that would allow the client to make sense of their surroundings in a way that establishes a skillset. "...the true reconciliation (which does not abolish modern subjective freedom) has to recognize how this disintegration is in itself already its opposite, a force of integration. Reconciliation is thus radically *immanent:* it implies a shift of perspective with regard to what first appeared as disintegration."[89] The dissolution of the self and the castration through the splitting of the self-subject through word may have an effect where the client feels weakened or frightened to not only reveal themselves, but to insufficiently reveal themselves. To tell a dream is to recount a surreal landscape with words, as if I was to type and describe the Mona Lisa. The oceanic enjoyment of the landscape would be somewhat missing, but what would be present is what in the Mona Lisa was important to me. In other words, the splitting through speech negates the Freudian intoxicated oceanic feeling, but allows for a free-associative unknotting of the signifying object's phenomenological structure based on what is psychically relevant to the therapeutic subject.

Nothing intoxicatingly oceanic makes it out of the near-future of Hegelian free-association in the room, but nothing needs to. This is not to say the therapeutic processing won't still have an effect of oceanic relaxation at revelations and unknotting of sinthome, but the added splitting of the subject through phenomenological free-association should allow for the client to take a sober outlook as a cutting expertise is crafted for future stimuli picked up by their neurological sensory input stations. Žižek writes further on the Hegelian method, "...it differentiates itself from itself, positing its otherness, and then again overcomes the difference—the entire movement is *its own* movement."[90] This in relating to the material societal economy can be extrapolated to the libidinal economy, "the 'truth' of its relating to its otherness is its self-relating, in its self-movement, capital retroactively 'sublates' its own material conditions, changing them into subordinate moments of its own 'spontaneous expansion'— in pure Hegelese, it posits its own presuppositions."[91] In the economic sphere, this capitalistic method of adjustment may leave the person left to fend for themselves on the fringes high and dry, but in the case of the individual psyche where one is only dealing with one's own economy of Understanding and Reason through various forms of ego-identification as well as projection into the Other. "In Hegel's idealism, negativity, alterity, and difference are asserted, but only as subordinate secondary moments serving their opposite—the absolute Subject re-appropriates all otherness, 'sublating' it into a moment of own self-meditation."[92] The addition, or rather emphasis, of this Hegelian projection into the Other as well as the knowledge of an absolute Subject appropriating discourse is similar to the way that the savvy consumer ignored the car ad to buy a car but was sold on the experience of driving.

Chapter 14

Individuation, a Sublation Formation

Because one is never sure how one is seen, one is never certain of one's place in the symbolic order. How, exactly, are we being looked at? One never really knows who one is – despite all the cameras, files, media, and databases. A celebrity gamer in one place is elsewhere just another kid. A famous jazz musician may have zero name recognition among economists. Someone with a million friends on MySpace may be no one at all to the rest of us. Facebook tries to help us out with this by supplying endless quizzes that promise to tell us who we really are – which lord of the rings character, which famous philosopher, which ferocious animal. Who one is in the socio-symbolic order is uncertain – and ever-changing. Žižek tags this flux and uncertainty as a decline in symbolic efficiency. In terms of Lacanian theory, the decline of symbolic efficiency is accompanied by a convergence between the imaginary and the Real. Imaginary identities sustained by the promise and provision of enjoyment replace symbolic identities.
Jodi Dean, Blog Theory[93]

Lacan's ideas were spoken, used in therapy with the individual, applied to social theory, then digitized for the modern age. This can be done backwards as well, and the disorder of contemporary digital capitalism flows backwards in temporal space through social theory, into dialog with the client, and spoken in seminar. Disjointed self becomes singular self and the self which is part of a system, and the argument of self and society being integrated as two separate pieces gets conflated with sublation of the social content into the individual psyche. In the context of psychotherapy, this is especially the case due to the fact that each client is intensely focused on, and their concepts and ideas are seen in contrast to the Jungian collective unconscious as individualistic, uniquely relating to them. But what uniquely relates to the client involves a discourse that is inevitably a conglomeration of subjects. These conglomerations of language and concepts meld together and the client integrates and abjects, forming their ego identity. What gets integrated begins to take on a totemic property, a symbolic point of reference for reverence.

What is abjected into the Other is treated with distain, or is simply looked at as alien, that which cannot be integrated into the ego ideal. "...consciousness first becomes explicitly a consciousness that comprehends [its object]. The result was the unconditioned universal, initial, in the negative and abstract sense that consciousness negated its one-sided Notions and abstracted them: in other words, it gave them up."[94] Similar to Lacan's mirror stage, the recognition of the self-consciousness gives us a sense of ego identity. We are always reconciling with the alien Other. We feign a sort of psychic centrism by stating that we are like the Other in certain ways and therefore we do not have this deep split in our conception of self because we recognize certain aspects in the interiority of another being that we have previously abjected from our own ego ideals, but this is what Žižek recognizes as pure death drive. We take the organ, and remove the body.[95]

Hegel continues, "But the result has, implicitly, a positive significance: in it, the unity of 'being-for-self' and 'being-for-another' is posited; in other words, the absolute antithesis is posited as a self-identical essence."[96] The subject that has been integrated into contemporary society thus must be capable of forming a singular identity which involves both the being-for-self and being-for-other. **The liberalized psyche thus is jolted back and forth between ideals with no symbolic order that is consistent; the psyche needs an ideal set that can only lead to a being-for-nothing. The root of depression is a detached nature from the symbolic order because it is empty in the fact that** it is arbitrary. However, when one fails to take the sublation of the surrounding society into the fold of their ego identity, the entire house of cards of significance inside the psyche collapses, depression takes hold as liberalism manufactures discontenting Nietzschean drive alongside the totems of decency and human rights that it supposedly represents.

It is not news that if we are doing individual psychotherapy, we must take into account surrounding circumstances. But this truism should be looked at not as partial object where sometimes the patient is focusing on the self and other times the Other, but rather the self is a condition of sublation into the various totemic practices of family, philosophy, politics, law, love, various social orders all playing off each other. The values are put in some order that resembles self interest inside the client, but cognitive dissonance reigns due to the impossibility of a singular belief set ruling over all these domains effectively. It would be like a total denial of materialism in the favor of notions based solely on a singular narrative of an epoch. "At first sight, this seems to concern only the form of the moments in reciprocal relation but 'being-for-self' and 'being-for-another' are the *content* itself as well, since the antithesis in its truth can have no other nature than the one yielded in the result, viz. that the content taken in perception to be true, belongs in fact only to the form, in the unity of which it is dissolved." [97] In other words, in the disunity of the self and other, a dialectic is formed.

The purpose of this Hegelian type of analysis into the formation of the absolute self in terms of clinical psychotherapy is that the dialectic process of sublation or integration of the external civilization does more than just discontent the subject, but is in fact the entire mechanism in which the subject decides on its desire. In other words, the context of the signifiers produced by the client, whether abjected into the Other or taken into the ego ideal, provide a framework for desire that is far from any sort of A=A proposition. "What comes first is the lack: the incestuous

Object of desire is always missing, it eludes the subject's grasp, all that desire can catch are the metonymies of the Thing, never the Thing itself."[98] When metaphor is added to an already abstracted Hegelian notion of the individual subjective being, things become more conflated. But this conflation of self, Other, abjection and metonymy (metonymy being an unavoidable accidental metaphor, extremely present in psychotic speech, but present in all speech to some degree) is the only way in which the wealth of information can be processed by the subject.

However, this repeated failure to reach the Thing can be inverted into success if the source of enjoyment is defined not as reaching the Thing, but as satisfaction brought about by the repeated effort to arrive at it. This brings us to the Freudian drive, whose true aim is not its goal (object), but the repeated attempt to reach it (for example, what brings satisfaction in the oral drive is not its object [milk], but the repeated act of sucking). We can thus conceive curvature, its circular movement, as ontologically secondary, as a way of turning the failure of desire into success.[99]

Individuation and the impossible freedom from sublating the self into the exterior reality as Hegel would put it, or the opposite (the exterior becoming the working processes of the individual) in the psychoanalytic sense is a project doomed to failure. In that individuation is doomed to failure, it is immortal in the psyche because it is a quest which has no end. From the traditional institutional man's view, this impossible quest producing jouissance due to its being unreachable is also what makes revolutionaries so detestable; the revolutionary seems to be demanding something that is impossible for their own enjoyment. This is why the necessity for Žižek's parallax view covered earlier is necessary to understand the mechanisms of lack, desire, individuation and sublation.

Yes, again, the relationship between historical and dialectical materialism is that of a parallax: they are substantially the same, the shift from the one to the other is purely one of perspective. It introduces topics like death drive, the 'inhuman' core of the human, which reach beyond the horizon of the collective praxis of humanity; the gap between historical and dialectical materialism is thus asserted as inherent to humanity itself, as the gap between humanity and its own inhuman excess.[100]

Žižek writes about Hegel's attempt to pick apart and rationally extract a core of the object in order to create a phenomenological investigation of the object or externality. Once this is done, the externality becomes the method of pulling on the observer into the framework of itself, and thus when the therapeutic subject feels they are pulling apart the framework, they are in fact delving inside and becoming sublated by the framework. The negation of the individual in this manner that pulls the subject into the externality is ironically the process of individuation that forms the ego ideal.

Individual therapy can seem like a contradiction in terms due to the sublated integration into systems which the therapeutic subject believes to be separate from rather than subsuming the role of the carrier of the system in which they are entering; however, individuation as a concept does not just disappear from the landscape. The Žižekian that is Hegelian-Lacanian therapeutic subject can thus be taken through the therapeutic process by means of their own sublation into the realms of their master signifiers.

One might say what is said of the divided kingdom, that any conception of the unity of the psyche, of the supposed totalizing, synthesizing psyche perishes (in the elaborate level of the real). Lastly—in these first stages of the experience in which remembering is gradually substituted for itself and approaches even nearer to a focus, or center, in which every event seems to be under an obligation to yield itself..."[101]

The necessity for the Lacanian viewpoint is not an aesthetic choice, but rather a tangible acceptance of the parallax, or the slipping ground in which one is viewing the psychic material. The repeating of master signifiers which reveal the knot is the only way to access the symbols of the unconscious which represent the sinthome of the client which is stuck in various registers. The pulling of the sinthome across the various perspectives of analytic inquiry via the master signifiers as jumping off points allows the analyst to take into account the center-less nature of the therapeutic subject's discourse. The ego ideal is a center, but then again what is abjected into the Other could also be framed as a center. Conscious thoughts could be the center. But these would all be incorrect assessments of the picture. Signifiers are important pieces because they are the beginning of mazes, not full pictures.

Chapter 15

Opening, Castling, Trading Off Pieces and Moving into the Endgame (The Proposed Therapeutic Structural System)

It would seem that the psychoanalyst, if he is simply to help the subject, must be spared this pathology, which, as we see, depends on nothing less than an iron-clad law. This is why people imagine that a psychoanalyst should be a happy man. Indeed, is it not happiness that people ask him for, and how could he give it, commonsense asks, if he does not have a bit of it himself.
Jacques Lacan, Ecrits[102]

One of the supposed advantages to cognitive approaches as opposed to psychodynamic approaches is that a cognitive approach can be reduced to a computer application, such as CCBT (Computerized Cognitive Behavioral Therapy) and the essence of the treatment is still there. This gives it the illusion of an objectivity, but of course it is not an objectivity because the method inscribes what will be treated on and the philosophy of the endgame of this hyper-constructivist approach. What is missing from any purely computerized model[103] is the recognition of signifiers, their meaning, their register and how to apply them in psychotherapy. This basic structural outline modeled after stages in the chess game will provide a template for people interested in this Žižekian (Hegelian-Lacanian) therapeutic philosophy and methodology.

Opening: In chess as in psychotherapy, the first player's very first move determines the entirety of the set of moves to be played in the rest of the game. The queen pawn being moved creates a more positional game or densely structured game, the King pawn a more dynamic game. In the same way, the initial move of the therapist determines the course of the treatment. In the Hegelian sense, it is also a negation of what the therapeutic process will not be aimed at. For the opening, whatever method gets the client talking about life information the most and providing signifiers. "What did you do this week?" turns into, "Oh what did you think about that activity?" turns into, "What about the person you did that activity with?" as a rough example. Throughout the process of this, keywords are given to the therapist that illuminate the knot around which symptom has swallowed itself up to be repressed and unexamined, and most importantly, unfelt by the client.

> It is in the subject's reduplication by the signifier that we find the mainspring...articulating itself ever anew, in the unconscious. A minimum composition of the battery of signifiers suffices to institute in the signifying chain a duplicity that re-covers his reduplication as a subject, and it is [through] this redoubling of the subject of speech that the unconscious as such finds a way to become articulated— namely, in a medium that is only apperceived by being perceived as just as stupid as a cryptography without a cipher."[104]

The cipher that the therapist has is the knowledge of how signifiers interact as batteries, and how themes can link through the unconscious which is structured linguistically. Links are created that reveal themselves to be surprisingly coherent even though the therapeutic subject was not thinking consciously about making the link. This is the information that it is up to the therapist to parse out and have the client further examine.

Castling: I would like to assure chess aficionados that yes, I understand castling is technically still part of opening theory. However, there is a specific parallel that castling has to the process of somehow making sense of the signifier batteries that are being delivered via psychotherapy. The client's defense mechanisms are propped up by master signifiers. Knots are tied around the sinthome and assemblages of meaning are presented to the therapist. This stage would not necessarily be a great challenging of the client's ego through the subversion of the analytic discourse; rather, the therapist may in fact use this moment to elicit even more ego structure and defenses propped up by master signifiers and repeated themes given by the client. This is the time that the therapist can use to gauge the client's tone and begin to match up some patterns of speech with them, begin to speak in the client's language. Through common-sense logic there is a falseness to this, but the opposite is also the case because it allows for an understanding and a bridge to be formed through client and therapist that would not be able to form otherwise. Through the arguable empty structure which is nonetheless thought out and placed there for a reason, the content which holds significance is able to cross over from client to therapist through the vector of speech. **During this process of client uncovering of their ego ideal, unconscious cognitive dissonances are recognized by the therapist and the client. The major themes are mapped into values by the therapist.** Lacan describes his linguistic modeling of discourse "like an apparatus. You should, at least, get the idea that it could be used as a lever, as a pair of pliers, that it can be screwed down, assembled in one way or another." [105] Here the therapist is put in the position of a type of mechanic. This may in fact put the therapist in the position of assuming a discourse and risks putting the therapist from the position of the analyst to one of the Hegelian master. This is not to say the therapist rules over the client, but merely presupposes to create this structure out of signifiers and show them to the client, with the statement along the lines of, "it's okay to have values which contradict, but that is the point in which we must make decisions from." The therapist then becomes a bit of an imposition, but only insofar as they are an instrument or, as Lacan puts it so well, for the new era for political discourse which we find ourselves in, "And the master subsequently appears only as the instrument, the magnificent Cuckold of history." [106]

Trading Off Pieces: It is a misconception that a client comes into therapy for happiness. More accurately, they come into therapy for a movement in a direction where life becomes more sustainable, enjoyable, less painful. This is not the same as happiness. It could, for instance, make a client very happy to ritualistically cut their wrists. The definition of happiness is so broad that it is almost meaningless. What has more objective truth to it is that the client comes to therapy for a change. When a client feels worse coming out of therapy, it can be part of the process. When the client comes out feeling happy, magnifíque! (they might think) it surely is working. What is unacceptable is, "the client sees no change." Another way of putting this is, "I have been working with the client for 2 months and their mental state is the same" is seen as much more unacceptable than, "I have been working with a client for 2 months and they seem to be sullener in the room." This can be many times truthfully put down to the fact that the client is suddenly, ritualistically confronting unresolved trauma and neuroses. This is not necessarily resolved in eight sessions. Even brief therapy consists usually of ten sessions.

The trade off is the actions which prioritize certain methods of thinking, deciding, that is irrational in that it causes the client more pain than they are willing to bear. Conflict between the client's values are inevitable, but the way that these conflicts arise when choosing how to interact as a sublated subject is able to shift. This is the primary movement. The knots have been examined and the signifiers have been strung out, and the client is able to examine the significance of the master signifiers which repeat in their psychotherapy. Once the client can do this they are able to examine how they want to approach future tests of the sinthome. This creates a bit of a yes/no binary that works as a Žižekian parallax which is always shifting the perspective of the decision. While there is no false, stable cognitive ground, the client nonetheless garners a knowledge of themselves and an ability to interact with their own signifiers in a meaningful way. The matheme $\{ø>1\}->\{1>ø\}$ as described earlier in the book, where $\{ø\}$ represents the void of the inaccessibility to the subjectivity of the Other which to the therapeutic subject is the therapist. $\{1\}$ represents the client who has access to themselves and thus represents the constitutive entity of the therapeutic subject. $\{->\}$ is "The Therapy," which is moving toward making the client able to not externalize the process of the examining of the knot which, with their signifiers, resides and creates meaning for the therapeutic subject. The exchanging of pieces is the movement toward the end of the therapeutic process.

Endgame: The final step in the therapeutic process involves the mapping of what can be termed on a microcosm level, event. Event here is anything that causes significant movement in the client's psyche. Once the client has insight into their values and the significance of certain signifiers, they can build an active knowledge and application set which continually processes new event outside of the therapist's office. Rather than just coping with feelings of discomfort, the client is able to use their newfound rationality. This is a much more Hegelian end of the process than a traditional Lacanian method, and it is in essence taking Hegel at his word, "What is rational is actual; and what is actual is rational." [107] But to stop with this statement would be insufficient, because what constitutes the rational and the actual in the therapeutic sense is the dialectic between the sinthome and microcosmic event.

The endgame in the Žižekian system is ultimately the algorithm. But an algorithm cannot just be given to a client by the therapist. The client has to go through the process of psychotherapy, recognize where they have knotted and repressed their discomfort under the guise of certain signifiers, then they must have the wherewithal to somehow change their relationship to their past, present and future. The psychotherapeutic process should be the therapist rendering themselves moot, in that the client should have the ability to recognize the significance of signifier and event, having examined the sinthome and what is knotted inside of them. This is not to say that the client slips into the delusion of the individual sans externality. Hegel's reproach of the individual mindset, "It is not the thing which is excellent, it is I who am excellent and master of both law and thing; I merely play with them as with my own caprice, and in this ironic consciousness in which I let the highest of things perish, I merely enjoy myself," is mitigated by the recognition of sublation to event. Event is determined by the externality of the client's world in which they inhabit.

There is no more Kaiser, but a client being yanked around by contemporary capitalism through the ringer now has a partial defense against this in what Hegel determined to be worthless on its own, this individual self-given authority. This approach is not quite Hegelian; the evil of subsumption to individual essence and microcosmic event alongside the unwillingness to recognize an authoritarian capitalist state would not be inline with Hegel's thinking. The trust in the conscious mind to recognize its own master signifiers in session is more heavy-handed than Lacan's Freudian analysis, but is nonetheless heavily informed by Lacan. The approach can only be called Žižekian in theory. There is a heroism in the individual who masters some sort of approach but also totally misses the point which Žižek seems to; simultaneously disgusted with and be pulled toward, staring at

Ayn Rand and Stalin with equal wonder and disgust that can only be termed, "Lacanian."

Žižek concretizes Lacan's theory of perversion as follows. "Perversion, at its most fundamental, resides in the formal structure of how the pervert relates to truth and speech. The pervert claims direct access to some figure of the Big Other... so that, dispelling all the ambiguity of language, he is able to act directly as the instrument of the Big Other's will." [108] A tempting mislabeling of this therapeutic proposition would be, "A Pervert's Guide to Slavoj Žižek," but it is not Žižek's will or his wishes for his theory that clinicians need to be concerned about (and it's not quite clear what these wishes could possibly be anyway). It is his accuracy in assessing phenomena, and the way a sinthome knot can be examined and treated.

This book is for the therapeutic subject who suffers and doesn't have the skill set yet to know what to do about it. This book can be read backwards and forwards and in no particular order depending on the interest of the reader. It is a continuing skill set of application to new microcosmic event for individual therapeutic subjects, and this process is not tied up in any particular ending.

Endnotes

1 Jacques Lacan, *The Other Side of Psychoanalysis, The Seminar of Jacques Lacan Book XVII* (Translator Russell Grigg), p.126, (2007)

2 Žižek discusses Freud's theory of "the ego not being master of its own house" through various films, specifically mentioning this Freudian theory as it relates to "Psycho"

3 S Phiennes (Director), *Pervert's Guide to Cinema* (2006)

4 G Millar (Director), *Rendez-vous Chez Lacan* (2011)

5 In the same place

6 Jacques Lacan, *The Other Side of Psychoanalysis, The Seminar of Jacques Lacan Book XVII* (Translator Russell Grigg), p.73 (2007)

7 Jacques Lacan, *Ecrits* (Seminar 1, translation by Bruce Fink), p.201, WW Norton and Company, 2006

8 Jacques Lacan, *Anxiety* (Seminar 10, Translation AR Price, Editor Jacques-Alain Miller), p.153-154, Polity Press, 2014

9 Aaron Beck, *Cognitive Therapy and the Emotional Disorders*, p.7, Meridian, 1979

10 Jacques Lacan, *Anxiety* (Seminar 10, Translation AR Price, Editor Jacques-Alain Miller), p.298, Polity Press, 2014

11 Slavoj Žižek, *Event*, p.42, Penguin Books Ltd, 2014

12 GWF Hegel, *The Philosophy of Right*, p.182, Cambridge University Press, 1991

13 Ludwig Wittgenstein, *Philosophical Investigations*, p.149, The Macmillan Company, 1958

14 Slavoj Žižek, *The Parallax View*, p.320, The MIT Press, 2006

15 Slavoj Žižek, *The Parallax View*, p.320, The MIT Press, 2006

16 Nick Land, *Meltdown*, 1994

17 Slavoj Žižek, *Event*, p.58, Penguin Books Ltd, 2014

18 Jacques Lacan, *Seminar VII: The Ethics of Psychoanalysis, 1959-1960*, p.139-140, Tavistock/Routledge, 1992

19   Jean-Paul Sartre, *Existentialism*, p.54-55, Philosophical Library New York, 1947

20   Todd McGowan, "The Necessity of an Absolute Misunderstanding: Why Hegel Has So Many Misreaders," *Slavoj Žižek and Dialectical Materialism*, p.48, Palgrave Macmillan, 2016

21   Jacques Lacan, *The Seminar of Jacques Lacan Book VIII Transference, 1960-1961* (Translator Cormac Gallagher), p.333

22   Sigmund Freud, *The Interpretation of Dreams*, p.437, Avon Books, 1965

23   Slavoj Žižek, "From Virtual Reality to the Virtualization of Reality," *Electronic Culture: Technology and Visual Representation*, Aperture, 1996

24   Jacques Lacan, *Anxiety* (Seminar 10, Translation AR Price, Editor Jacques-Alain Miller), p.86, Polity Press, 2014

25   Jacques Lacan, *The Otherside of Psychoanalysis, The Seminar of Jacques Lacan Book XVII* (Translator: Russell Grigg), p.80, WW Norton and Company, 2007

26   In the same place, p.172

27   "What do you want?"

28   Marsha M. Linehan, *DBT Skills Training Handouts and Worksheets (Second Edition)*, p.132-133, The Guildford Press, 2015

29   Jacques Lacan, *The Otherside of Psychoanalysis, The Seminar of Jacques Lacan Book XVII* (Translator Russell Grigg), p.101, WW Norton and Company, 2007

30   Danaides are described in a footnote in seminar 17 as the daughters of a king forced to marry their cousins, whom the daughters then killed: "the murderers were punished in the Underworld by having to fill leaky jars with water." In the same place, p.72

31   In the same place

32   Dale Carnegie, *How to Win Friends and Influence People*,

p.105, Pocket Books, 1998

33 Jacques Lacan, *The Otherside of Psychoanalysis, The Seminar of Jacques Lacan Book XVII* (Translator Russell Grigg), p.174, WW Norton and Company, 2007

34 "Unemployed, or living in slums and in other interstices of the public space," Editors Costas Douzinas and Slavoj Žižek, *The Idea of Communism*, "How to Begin from the Beginning", p.226, Slavoj Žižek, Verso Books, 2010

35 In the same place

36 GWF Hegel, *Phenomenology of Mind*, p.61, Blackmask Online, 2001

37 Jacques Lacan, *Ecrits* (Seminar 1, translation by Bruce Fink), p.201, WW Norton and Company, 2006

38 Claude Levi-Strauss, *Totemism*, p.68, Beacon Press, 1963

39 In the same place, p.58

40 Sigmund Freud, *Collected Papers Volume 1*, "The Psycho-Analytic Method," p.270-271, Basic Books, 1959

41 Slavoj Žižek, "Signs from the Future," Lecture from May 14 2012

42 Jacques Lacan, *Ecrits* (Seminar 1, translation by Bruce Fink), p.59, WW Norton and Company, 2006

43 Aaron Beck, *Cognitive Therapy and the Emotional Disorders*, p.137, Meridian, 1979

44 Jacques Lacan, *Seminar VII: The Ethics of Psychoanalysis, 1959-1960*, p.104, Tavistock/Routledge, 1992

45 Jacques Lacan, *Seminar VII: The Ethics of Psychoanalysis, 1959-1960*, p.44, Tavistock/Routledge, 1992

46 In the same place, p.168

47 Slavoj Žižek, *First as Tragedy, then as Farce*, p.37, Verso, 2009

48 Alain Badiou, *Being and Event*, p.161, Continuum, 2005

49 In the same place, p.169

50 Slavoj Žižek, *First as Tragedy, then as Farce*, p.53, Verso, 2009

51 Slavoj Žižek, *In Defense of Lost Causes*, p.384, Verso, 2009

52 GWF Hegel, *Hegel's Logic*, p.166, Oxford University Press,

1975

53 Jacques Lacan, *The Seminar of Jacques Lacan, VIII Transference*, p.329, Lacan in Ireland (undated)

54 Suzanne Bernard and Bruce Fink (eds.), *Reading Seminar XX: Lacan's Major Work on Love, Knowledge, and Feminine Sexuality*, Slavoj Žižek, "The Real of Sexual Difference," p.59-60, State University of New York Press, Albany, 2002

55 Dylan Evans, *An introductory dictionary of Lacanian psychoanalysis*, p.96, Routledge, 1996

56 Marsha M Linehan, *DBT Skills Training Handouts and Worksheets (Second Edition)*, p.9, The Guildford Press, 2015

57 Jacques Lacan, *Ecrits* (Seminar 1, translation by Bruce Fink), p.691, WW Norton and Company, 2006

58 Sigmund Freud, *Collected Papers Volume 2*, "The Psycho-Analytic Method," p.170-171, Basic Books, 1959

59 S Phiennes (Director), *Pervert's Guide to Ideology* (2011)

60 In the same place

61 Jacques Lacan, *Ecrits* (Seminar 1, translation by Bruce Fink), p.85, WW Norton and Company, 2006

62 In the same place, p.16

63 Bruce Fink, *Lacan to the Letter: Reading Ecrits Closely*, p.43-44, University of Minnesota Press, 2004

64 In the same place, p.66

65 Slavoj Žižek, *Tarrying with the Negative: Kant, Hegel, and the Critique of Ideology*, p.72, Duke University Press, 1993

66 In the same place, p.73

67 Jacques Lacan, *The Seminar of Jacques Lacan XXIII: Le Sinthome*, p.11, Lacan Online (undated)

68 In the same place, p.47

69 Bruce Fink, *Lacan to the Letter: Reading Ecrits Closely*, p.80, University of Minnesota Press, 2004

70 Jacques Lacan, *The Seminar of Jacques Lacan XXIII: Le Sinthome*, p.54, Lacan Online (undated)

71 Slavoj Žižek, *In Defense of Lost Causes*, p.350, Verso, 2009

72   Jacques Lacan, *The Seminar of Jacques Lacan XXIII: Le Sinthome*, p.46, Lacan Online (undated)

73   In the same place

74   Jacques Lacan, *Seminar VII: The Ethics of Psychoanalysis, 1959-1960*, p.75, Tavistock/Routledge, 1992

75   In the same place

76   Jacques Lacan, *Ecrits* (Seminar 1, translation by Bruce Fink), p.201, WW Norton and Company, 2006

77   In the same place, p.202

78   In the same place, p.366

79   Slavoj Žižek, *How to Read Lacan*, pp.91 and 123, WW Norton and Company, 2006

80   In the same place, p.93

81   S Phiennes (Director), *Pervert's Guide to Ideology* (2011)

82   Slavoj Žižek, *How to Read Lacan*, p.25, WW Norton and Company, 2006

83   Jacques Lacan, *Ecrits* (Seminar 1, translation by Bruce Fink), p.285, WW Norton and Company, 2006

84   In the same place, p.125

85   In the same place, p.126

86   Slavoj Žižek, *Less than Nothing: Hegel and the Shadow of Dialectical Materialism*, p.197, Verso, 2012

87   Orgone is the non-existence substance postulated to exist by Wilhelm Reich that could be accumulated via sitting in a box made out of a certain combination of wood and metal layering.

88   Slavoj Žižek, *Less than Nothing: Hegel and the Shadow of Dialectical Materialism*, p.242, Verso, 2012

89   In the same place

90   In the same place, p.250

91   In the same place

92   In the same place, p.262

93   Jodi Dean, *Blog Theory*, p.57, Polity Press, 2010

94   GWF Hegel, *Phenomenology of Spirit*, p.80, Oxford University

Press, 1977

95   S Phiennes (Director), *Pervert's Guide to Cinema* (2006) (the scene where our hero of this writing Slavoj is on a canoe, talking about the Cheshire Cat smile)

96   GWF Hegel, *Phenomenology of Spirit*, p.80, Oxford University Press, 1977

97   In the same place

98   Slavoj Žižek, *Less than Nothing: Hegel and the Shadow of Dialectical Materialism*, p.376, Verso, 2012

99   In the same place

100 In the same place, p.393

101 Jacques Lacan, *Four Fundamental Concepts of Psychoanalysis*, p.51, WW Norton and Company, 1998

102 Jacques Lacan, *Ecrits* (Seminar 1, translation by Bruce Fink), p.513, WW Norton and Company, 2006

103 As of New Year's Day, 2018

104 Jacques Lacan, *Ecrits* (Seminar 1, translation by Bruce Fink), p.595, WW Norton and Company, 2006

105 Jacques Lacan, *The Other Side of Psychoanalysis, The Seminar of Jacques Lacan Book XVII* (Translator Russell Grigg), p.169, WW Norton and Company, (2007)

106 In the same place, p.171

107 GWF Hegel, *The Philosophy of Right*, p.20, Cambridge University Press, 1991

108 Slavoj Žižek, *How to Read Lacan*, p.116, WW Norton and Company, 2006

Zero Books

CULTURE, SOCIETY & POLITICS

Contemporary culture has eliminated the concept and public figure of the intellectual. A cretinous anti-intellectualism presides, cheer-led by hacks in the pay of multinational corporations who reassure their bored readers that there is no need to rouse themselves from their stupor. Zer0 Books knows that another kind of discourse – intellectual without being academic, popular without being populist – is not only possible: it is already flourishing. Zer0 is convinced that in the unthinking, blandly consensual culture in which we live, critical and engaged theoretical reflection is more important than ever before.

If you have enjoyed this book, why not tell other readers by posting a review on your preferred book site.

Recent bestsellers from Zero Books are:

In the Dust of This Planet
Horror of Philosophy vol. 1
Eugene Thacker
In the first of a series of three books on the Horror of
Philosophy, *In the Dust of This Planet* offers the genre of horror
as a way of thinking about the unthinkable.
Paperback: 978-1-84694-676-9 ebook: 978-1-78099-010-1

Capitalist Realism
Is there no alternative?
Mark Fisher
An analysis of the ways in which capitalism has presented itself
as the only realistic political-economic system.
Paperback: 978-1-84694-317-1 ebook: 978-1-78099-734-6

Rebel Rebel
Chris O'Leary
David Bowie: every single song. Everything you want to know,
everything you didn't know.
Paperback: 978-1-78099-244-0 ebook: 978-1-78099-713-1

Cartographies of the Absolute
Alberto Toscano, Jeff Kinkle
An aesthetics of the economy for the twenty-first century.
Paperback: 978-1-78099-275-4 ebook: 978-1-78279-973-3

Malign Velocities
Accelerationism and Capitalism
Benjamin Noys
Long listed for the Bread and Roses Prize 2015, *Malign Velocities* argues against the need for speed, tracking acceleration as the symptom of the ongoing crises of capitalism.
Paperback: 978-1-78279-300-7 ebook: 978-1-78279-299-4

Meat Market
Female Flesh under Capitalism
Laurie Penny
A feminist dissection of women's bodies as the fleshy fulcrum of capitalist cannibalism, whereby women are both consumers and consumed.
Paperback: 978-1-84694-521-2 ebook: 978-1-84694-782-7

Poor but Sexy
Culture Clashes in Europe East and West
Agata Pyzik
How the East stayed East and the West stayed West.
Paperback: 978-1-78099-394-2 ebook: 978-1-78099-395-9

Romeo and Juliet in Palestine
Teaching Under Occupation
Tom Sperlinger
Life in the West Bank, the nature of pedagogy and the role of a university under occupation.
Paperback: 978-1-78279-637-4 ebook: 978-1-78279-636-7

Sweetening the Pill
or How we Got Hooked on Hormonal Birth Control
Holly Grigg-Spall
Has contraception liberated or oppressed women? *Sweetening the Pill* breaks the silence on the dark side of hormonal contraception.
Paperback: 978-1-78099-607-3 ebook: 978-1-78099-608-0

Why Are We The Good Guys?
Reclaiming your Mind from the Delusions of Propaganda
David Cromwell
A provocative challenge to the standard ideology that Western power is a benevolent force in the world.
Paperback: 978-1-78099-365-2 ebook: 978-1-78099-366-9

Readers of ebooks can buy or view any of these bestsellers by clicking on the live link in the title. Most titles are published in paperback and as an ebook. Paperbacks are available in traditional bookshops. Both print and ebook formats are available online.

Find more titles and sign up to our readers' newsletter at http://www.johnhuntpublishing.com/culture-and-politics

Follow us on Facebook
at https://www.facebook.com/ZeroBooks

and Twitter at https://twitter.com/Zer0Books